About the Author

ARIEL LEVE is an award-winning journalist who worked as a senior writer on contract with the London *Sunday Times Magazine* from 2003 to 2011. Her work has appeared in *The Guardian*, *The Telegraph*, the *Financial Times*, *Wall Street Journal*, *Esquire*, and other publications. She is the author of *It Could Be Worse, You Could Be Me*, a collection of her columns, and coauthor (with Robin Morgan) of *1963: The Year of the Revolution*.

"Leve writes of learning to be constantly on guard, living 'an abbreviated life,' and how she finally found her way out. Hers is an unsentimental tale, both cautionary and heartening."   —BBC.com

"Exquisitely written."   —Lynn Barber, *Sunday Times* (London)

"Leve's prose is soulful, cryptic, musing."
   —Sheila Weller, *New York Observer*

"Leve . . . writes in beautiful, staccato sentences and weaves her own story together masterfully."   —*Evening Standard* (London)

"Unflinching in detail."   —*Vogue*

"Leve's powerful story of surviving her brutal childhood demonstrates that contentment can be found."   —*Publishers Weekly*

"A candid rendering of pain and survival."   —*Kirkus Reviews*

"*An Abbreviated Life* adds a harrowing chapter to the great human tragi-comedy called 'We Don't Get To Choose Our Parents.' Ariel Leve's extremely readable memoir is, at its heart, a story about surviving childhood—a trick we must all perform. As such, even in its raw extremes, her story is a universal one."   —Richard Ford

"The staccato style of this searing memoir enhances the harshness and emotional power of what is a frightening story by a brave author, who resolutely describes herself as 'a long-distance runner through the canyon of childhood'—a modest understatement. This is the story of an endangered childhood, tyrannized by an out-of-control and fear-inspiring mother. This book is an unstinting portrayal of psychological abuse, both insightful and precisely told."   —John Irving

"Sometimes, a child is born to a parent who can't be a parent, and, like a seedling in the shade, has to grow toward a distant sun. Ariel Leve's spare and powerful memoir will remind us that family isn't everything—kindness and nurturing are."   —Gloria Steinem

"Out of a childhood that seems just about impossible to have survived, Ariel Leve has written a haunting, indelible story that becomes its own form of redemption. This is an act of bravery that strikes me not only as a literary achievement, but a human one."   —Dani Shapiro

AN ABBREVIATED LIFE

An Abbreviated Life

A MEMOIR

Ariel Leve

HARPER ● PERENNIAL

NEW YORK ● LONDON ● TORONTO ● SYDNEY ● NEW DELHI ● AUCKLAND

First U.S. hardcover edition published in 2016 by HarperCollins Publishers.

HarperCollins books may be purchased for educational, business, or sales promotional use. For information, please e-mail the Special Markets Department at SPsales@harpercollins.com.

FIRST HARPER PERENNIAL EDITION PUBLISHED 2017.

Designed by William Ruoto

Library of Congress Cataloging-in-Publication Data

Names: Leve, Ariel, 1968– author.
Title: An abbreviated life : a memoir / Ariel Leve.
Description: First edition. | New York : Harper, 2016.
Identifiers: LCCN 2015050966 | ISBN 9780062269454 (hardback)
Subjects: LCSH: Leve, Ariel, 1968– | Leve, Ariel, 1968—Psychology. | Leve, Ariel, 1968—Family. | Journalists—Great Britain—Biography. | BISAC: BIOGRAPHY & AUTOBIOGRAPHY / Personal Memoirs. | PSYCHOLOGY / General.
Classification: LCC PN5123.L43 A3 2016 | DDC 070.92—dc23 LC record available at http://lccn.loc.gov/2015050966

ISBN 978-0-06-226946-1 (pbk.)

19 20 21 OV/LSC 10 9 8 7 6 5 4 3 2

AN ABBREVIATED LIFE

1

I am on the other side of the planet from New York, twenty-five meters beneath sea level. The fish are phosphorescent. There is coral shaped like a brain. Other coral reminds me of mushrooms. I am silently passing over the swaying tubes, the pointy structures, my head tilted down so that I can see through my mask as I take in the scene and glide over the surface of the moon, sand dunes and mazes, rigid stony corals and silky ones that look like teardrops. The only sound is of bubbles. I watch as they float up toward the surface, a place I have no desire to return to.

Here, underwater, I am free. Unleashed from history. My mother will never find me. I am untraceable. I equalize the pressure and descend even deeper.

MY MOTHER SAYS, "When I'm dead, you will be all alone because your father doesn't want you. You know that, right?"

I am six years old, an only child.

She is naked in front of the white porcelain sink putting on eye shadow, and I am seated on top of the toilet seat, perched on the lid, watching as she gets ready to go out for the evening.

She says, "Just remember that and treat me nicely."

2

That same year, I stopped speaking for six months. My mother sent me to a psychiatrist. He put me on Valium and we played checkers. I stopped speaking because Kiki, the woman who had looked after me since I was born, who had endured my mother's behavior, my father's departure, who'd seen to it that I was clothed and fed and attended school, the woman I was attached to the way a child should be to her mother, died on a plane while sitting next to me. It was 1974 and we were returning to New York after a visit with my father, who lived in Bangkok.

I remember we were seated in the middle of the plane, in the middle of a row. The neon-yellow oxygen mask fell from the ceiling. It looked like a Dixie cup dangling from a string. There was an announcement the pilot made asking if there was a doctor on the flight. I was moved to a different part of the plane and seated next to a stranger. There was an awareness that something alarming was going on. The plane made an emergency landing in Greenland so they could remove Kiki's body from the aircraft, and an airline representative from Lufthansa escorted me the rest of the way.

Kiki had suffered a stroke.

Later, when I started speaking again, I began to ask everyone for their phone number. I made people promise, if they were leaving, to tell me when we would see each other again. My mother decided I shouldn't go back to Thailand. She said if my father loved me, he wouldn't have moved so far away. But then she also said that he loved me more than anyone. I started to stutter. It disappeared when I was seven years old, and from then on, she let me return to see him once a year.

KIKI'S DEATH BECAME a mythological incident. I had little memory of the experience other than before and after. Order, then disorder. I was told about it as though I hadn't been there. An unfortunate occurrence. The time when Kiki died. The time when I stopped speaking. Plot points in the story that amounted to *one more thing*.

THE GRAVITRON IS a ride at amusement parks and carnivals. It is an enclosed circular machine with padded panels on the walls. When you step on this ride, you lean back against the panels. The ride begins to rotate and the centrifugal force removes the machine from the ground on a slant, so that you are experiencing the force three times the speed of gravity. The world spins around. You are tilted and you spin and you spin. And when you are through, you step off the ride, but even with your feet on the ground, the world is still spinning. Up is down. You can't find your balance.

Ihate you. I love you. You're a moron. I never said that. You're the most important person in the world to me. I wish you were never born. Your father left you because he's a selfish man who doesn't care about you. He's a wonderful father and you're lucky to have him. You should be grateful. You should be happy. You're a liar—I never did that. You're jealous of me. You should be thanking your lucky stars to have me as your mother. What are you talking about—why are you making up these spiteful lies about me—I never did that. I never said that. What's wrong with you? You hate me. You always have and I feel very sorry for you.

I AM IN hiding. An emotional fugitive. I am trying to write a letter to my mother from here in Bali. A disconnection notice. A termination of service. I have revised this letter a dozen times. Staying one step ahead is essential. I am careful of the words. Frightened of the consequence. I am launching the separation grenade from ten thousand miles away so that when it detonates, I will be at a distance.

Can I write this letter? Can I send it?

·   ·   ·

IMAGINE SOMEONE LIES to you and about you. Imagine this person is your mother, whose job it is to provide safety, security, consistency, and love. "You're my sunshine," she says. "The love of my life."

But her love comes with conditions. You need to be able to give her what she needs first. You have to meet her demands. For attention, appreciation, company, and admiration. Anything else is unacceptable. But no matter how much you give, there will be a need for more. These are the terms. You were five. You were ten. You were twenty. You were forty. And at forty-five, something changed.

4

I had come to spend my forty-fifth birthday with my father, who lives in Bali. A few days later, I was taking a walk on the beach. I stopped at a hut with a thatched roof and a chalkboard out front—a surf and dive school that offered lessons.

SINCE I WAS five years old, my father has lived on the other side of the world. As an adult, I would be in New York and wonder what I would do if something happened to him. It would mean getting on a plane and flying for two days—as far as one can go without heading back—and navigating help for him in Southeast Asia, where resources are limited and efficiency is on a different timeline. I would not speak the language. It would be brutally hot—the kind of steamy heat that fosters inertia.

Now I live in the same place that he lives. It is the first time we have spent more than a few months together. I will ride my bicycle over to his house and we will talk and share and laugh and comfort each other.

I have escaped from New York and my mother. I dive in, past the tentacles of her reach.

· · ·

WHEN I MET Mario, before I knew we would have a story, he told me, "I want to take you diving and show you my world. The underwater world. A world without words."

He took my hand and I didn't want him to let go. I was afraid I would drift away.

THE FIRST TIME I went to his house, I couldn't find it. It is at the end of an unmarked road. "Pass the banana field and turn left," he had said. Though he lives in the same quiet coastal town as my father, his house is in a far more remote area, a place not easily accessible. It's on the "other side" of the bypass, the paved road that separates the expat community from where the locals live. Mario had given me the number of the house, but the number is not displayed. I stood on a dirt path and called him as the chickens walked past. "I'm lost," I said. There was no red pin-sized dot on the map. He appeared a few minutes later, barefoot, and led the way. To the house without a number on a road without a name.

MY MOTHER NEEDED me around. She could not be alone. One day she decided she would teach poetry to my fourth-grade class at the all-girls school I attended. She said that she missed me too much during the day. There was an announcement during homeroom: poetry would be on the curriculum in the new semester. It was a "special opportunity" twice a week—for my class only.

It was her first day of teaching and I was nervous. What would she wear? What would she say? Before I left that morning, I slipped a note under her bedroom door. She was still asleep and I worried she wouldn't notice it, so I knocked.

"Are you awake?" I asked. There was no response. I opened the door and stood on the wooden threshold that separated her room from the foyer. "You have to get up or you'll be late."

She rolled over without opening her eyes. "I'm up." I walked toward her until I reached the edge of her bed.

"Promise," I said, tugging on the blanket, "that you won't say certain words."

She didn't respond. I tugged again. "Promise me."

I went around to where her head was and held out the piece of paper with the word I didn't want her to use. Cocksucker. She loved that word.

"Don't say fuck either," I added. She was nodding. I put the paper down on the nightstand and placed the ashtray on top of it.

"Don't forget to brush your hair. And don't wear a nightgown."

My mother lived in nightgowns. She would wear them all the time. Sometimes they would be inside out, but she didn't care. Sometimes they would be sheer, but she didn't mind. She wore them everywhere. In the apartment, on the street, during the day—it didn't matter. One time she wore a pink flannel nightgown to Parents' Day. When I told her it was embarrassing, she got upset.

"Who cares what I wear!" she scoffed. "Don't be so vain."

I tried not to be vain.

She showed up that day wearing sweatpants (inside out) and a white T-shirt instead. The T-shirt was decorated with *Wonder Woman* stamped across her ample bosom. She wasn't wearing a bra.

"I'm Ariel's mommy," she announced cheerfully. "But you can call me Suzy."

She instructed everyone to stand up. My classmates pushed back the chairs from their desks and stood in the aisle.

"Before we begin, we need to warm up."

Oh no, I thought. Not the warm-up. But it was too late. She had begun the jumping jacks. Arms flapping, bosoms bouncing up and down, up and down.

MY CLASSMATES ADORED her. She chewed gum and told them stories about her life and all of her problems. She would ask their advice. Mostly, though, she would read her own poetry. Parents of the girls in the class complained. Someone had gone home and asked what a *vulva* was. Someone else had asked about *whore*. My classmate Christina's mother hit the roof. She didn't think these were appropriate topics for a nine-year-old. For me, these were not unusual words. Nor were the explanations of what they meant toned down in any way.

Elizabeth, whose father was a banker, lived on Park Avenue and was dyslexic. She had been left back a grade and couldn't bring herself to say Suzy because it was too informal; teachers had to be Miss or Mrs. My mother encouraged her to write because in poetry there were no mistakes. Her enthusiasm for instilling belief in a talent was powerful. "You *can* write," she would say. "You have something to say."

YEARS LATER, WHEN I was in my twenties, I ran into Elizabeth on the street. We stood for a few minutes on the corner of 83rd and Lexington. She had become a lawyer and she asked how my mother was. I gave my standard response: the same.

"She was a good teacher," Elizabeth recalled. And Christina, who later became a writer, told me, "Your mother said that I had a gift. I never forgot that."

5

There was my mother, Suzanne, the poet. There was my father, Harvey, who moved to Bangkok when I was five. There was Josie, who had the job of raising me after Kiki died. And there was Rita, my father's ex-girlfriend, who wrote to him every day after he left New York, and who gave me what was needed when it was needed the most.

Dear Harvey,

Here we go again with reports of horrors from 180 E. 79th St. Josie called last night to tell me that Ariel has been very sad and upset lately—especially since you left. Last week, Suzanne happened to be home when Ariel was getting ready for bed and promised to kiss her good night. Just before bedtime, Suzanne got on the phone and talked for an hour and a half. All the while, Ariel was calling out for her and crying. Usual story, I guess. The next day at school, Ariel wrote a story in class about running away.

She showed the story to her mother. Suzanne was angry and said, "Why did you write this? This isn't about me, is it?"

"Oh" was Ariel's reply. "It's just a story."

Suzanne insisted that Ariel change the story and Ariel

refused. After much arguing, Suzanne wore her down.
Ariel said she would change it to a dog running away.
Then Suzanne went out. But as soon as she got on the
elevator to leave, Ariel yelled out to no one in particular,

"I'm not changing my story! I'm not!"

Suzanne has since ordered Ariel not to write any more
stories. She's only to write poems. Suzanne said that when
Ariel has written lots of poems, she'll have them published.
Josie was upset after reading the story. She says Ariel is
very sad because Daddy didn't put her in his suitcase.
Your pal,

Rita

I DIDN'T CHANGE my story because my story was real. I
knew that at seven years old.

I CAN'T REMEMBER the first time my mother said she was
having a nervous breakdown, but throughout my childhood, these declarations were a regular occurrence. "I'm
having a nervous breakdown" was uttered with the routine
frequency of "I'm thirsty." Only instead of a flat statement,
it was a hysterical battle cry that demanded urgency.

"I'm cracking up!" my mother would frequently announce. "I'm going to end up in Bellevue. Is that what you want?"

The Bellevue psychiatric ward in Manhattan was her destiny if I wasn't careful. The message was: my behavior determined her sanity.

I needed to get out of her way. I had to stop playing, stop laughing—I was not respecting the fact that she was in crisis. She was going to jump out the window. Or off the roof. Sometimes this was followed with "Then you'll be happy."

6

It's brain damage. That's what she says. She's referring to me. She says it again. Brain damage. I have seen Emily, my therapist, on and off for the past seventeen years. I am in my early forties and I've returned to New York after living in London. Her office is on the ground floor of a residential building on the Upper West Side. I hear a pneumatic drill outside the window, cracking open the pavement. "Do you hear that?" I ask. She nods. There are hydrangeas on her desk.

I tell her I think of brain damage as causing people not to be able to walk or talk. Veterans. Stroke victims. Boxers. Football players. My tone is incredulous. She nods again, slower this time, in acknowledgment. "There are parts of your brain that did not develop the way they should have. And the way you function is a consequence." The brain is damaged. She says it again. She explains how children reflect the world they are raised in. Trauma, fear, and anxiety alters the brain as it is developing.

I stared at her, taking this in.

I wondered: how does a child build a foundation on quicksand?

BEING BORN WAS a game my mother loved to play. Maybe I was five, definitely six, possibly seven. I would be beckoned into her bedroom and she would be naked in her king-size bed under the sheets. The brass headboard was glistening from the sunlight that shone through the glass French doors that opened up onto her terrace.

"Let's play Being Born," she would announce. "I want to relive the happiest day of my life!"

She would laugh, giddy with excitement. I savored the opportunity to spend time with her. I had her attention focused on me, and that was a treat. I'd climb into bed with her and crawl under the sheets. We would play this game when I came home from school. I was still wearing my uniform. I'd take off my shoes and socks and the light blue pinafore would bunch up as I wriggled my way down to the part of the bed where I could be between her legs. She would spread her legs open, the soles of her bare feet on the bed, knees in the air, and I would curl up in a ball in between her bare thighs. She placed a pillow on top of her belly to create an exaggerated bump as she narrated the story of giving birth: the happiest day of her life.

"This is where you lived for nine months," she would begin, trailing off into a story about herself and what she was doing when she was pregnant. She would take me to the Russian Tea Room and eat borscht. "Then one day it was time for you to come out into the world!" She began the patterned breathing so that puffs of air would come out of her mouth, imitating the heaving sighs of giving birth. On the count of three, *pop!* The covers were yanked back and the bland air and bright daylight would rush back over me. I would enter the world and lie on her belly and she would hold me and rock me and smother me with kisses.

I RECALL THAT one time after school I had a classmate over. Danielle was, like me, one of the shortest girls in first grade. In the yearbook photos, we would be placed standing next to each other, always in the first row because of our height. Danielle lived in an apartment on Park Avenue South and her dog, a German shepherd, was named Frederick.

The names of my childhood friends' animals have stayed with me. I used to lie in bed at night and when the unfiltered shouting began, to block it out, instead of counting sheep, I would recite all the names that I could of my friends' pets.

(Later I learned this ability to dissociate was altering my brain.)

DANIELLE AND I were eating carrot sticks in the living room when the chance to play Being Born arose. My mother called out from her bedroom, "Come and spend some time with me!" We took turns. First I would be born; then it was Danielle's turn. Sometimes the birth would be loud and painful. Sometimes it would be effortless. We jumped up and down on the bed, waiting to go again. After several births in a row, my mother got bored or tired and made a phone call. The game ended.

After that day, Danielle was never allowed to come over again. I can imagine now the conversation with her mother when she went home. "What did you do at Ariel's house?"

"We got into bed," Danielle might have said. "With Ariel's mother, who was naked. Then she pretended to push us out through her vagina."

I HAD FORGOTTEN all about Being Born. In all my years of therapy, I'd never mentioned it. One day I asked Emily casually, "Did I ever tell you about being born?"

When I told her about the game, the look on her face frightened me. Being Born hadn't seemed at all significant until that moment. The wobbly look of shock that indicated this was not a normal game mothers play with their children.

"Do you realize that behavior was inappropriate?" Emily asked.

I hadn't. For me, it was a positive memory of a playful time. I received loving attention from my mother and this was the package it came in. It wasn't a titillating experience for her; it was her way of showing she cared. As I explained (and by default, defended) my mother's behavior, I had a fleeting understanding of invisible damage. And that there was no normal, only a calcified tolerance of abnormal.

7

Mario showed me a photo of his six-year-old twin daughters on his phone. They looked like little dolls: half Italian, half Chinese, with long brown hair and features that seemed impossibly flawless. I was asking him questions because I was curious. They were from a previous relationship. He was no longer with their mother.

Later, when our relationship started, I didn't consider what it would be like to be involved with a man who had children. But uncharacteristically, I didn't question it. I didn't analyze the pros and cons or think about how it would make me feel and where I would fit in. There was only a feeling that it wasn't an obstacle. They were part of his life and they would be a part of mine, too.

THE FIRST TIME I met them, I was uneasy. I couldn't tell them apart and was afraid of getting them mixed up. I didn't know how to talk to them. I wasn't confident about how to relate.

"Just be yourself," Mario said.

That's what I was worried about.

They weren't impressed. They had spent time with a woman he had been seeing before me and the attention I was giving them was comparatively more reserved. After our first meeting I asked him what they said.

"They don't know you yet. Give it time."

THREE MONTHS LATER, when I tell the girls I am going for a visit with my father, who lives fifteen minutes away, they look unhappy that I am leaving. Mario, whom I now live with, straddles a branch above us seventeen feet off the ground, using giant shears to clip the leaves off the Kupu Kupu tree. The leaves have the shape of butterfly wings.

"How long will you be gone for?" one of them asks.

"Not very long," I say. "I'll be back soon."

They both make a face. Expressions of disappointment.

"Maybe an hour at the most," I say. But as soon as I say this, I know it is not a comfort. I am leaving them and specifics of time do not soothe. They do not know how long one hour is or what that means. Absence is unpredictable.

I reassure them. "I'll be back before dinner."

"I'LL BE BACK," my mother says, "after dinner." She is on her way out for the evening.

I wait for her to return. The babysitter has been asked to sleep over. I know this means my mother might not come home.

"You promise you're sleeping here tonight?" I call out to her as she is getting on the elevator.

"Yes," my mother says. "I promise to be home after dinner."

In the morning I go to her bedroom to wake her up and she is not there. The bed is still made.

THE GIRLS BOTH run across the garden after me as I get on my bicycle. I open the green gate and they follow me out onto the black pebble road. They stand there, both of them shielding their eyes from the sun, seeing me off.

"I'm going to stay here and watch you ride away on your bicycle," one of them says. "Because I love you."

I pedal away for a few seconds and then stop. I get off the bike, flick the kickstand with my foot, and stand with both arms extended forward. This is the signal for a hug. The girls come running over and wrap their arms around my torso, one on either side. I pull them in tight. We embrace for a few seconds and then I lean down so that they can kiss me on the face. I kiss them back, several times, before taking off again on my bike.

MY MOTHER SAYS, "What kind of daughter doesn't want to kiss her own mother? How did I get such an unaffectionate child?"

I don't respond. Her ire doesn't change my mind. And I don't feel criminal.

When my mother kissed me, I wiped the kiss off my cheek. I used the back of my hand and wrinkled my nose. Her kisses were uncomfortable on my skin. She was wounded by this reaction. But it wasn't meant to punish her. It was an instinctive revolt. She responded by grasping me in her arms, suffocating me with kiss after kiss after kiss after kiss.

"Don't!" I protested, trying to disentangle from her clutch, like a cat that thrashes around when it doesn't want to be held. I knew, in a way that I couldn't articulate, her kisses weren't about me.

8

There is a black-and-white photograph of my mother and father, and I stare at it often. My mother is sitting in an upholstered armchair, on the edge of the cushion, poised to get up. My father sits on the arm of the chair, leaning forward, clasping her hand, believing in things he will later regret. In this picture my mother is in her early thirties, nearly fifteen years younger than I am now. I look at her face. It is a face I don't recognize. Serene and alluring. I want to talk to her, be her friend. Share a secret. Can you hear me? I would have liked to have known you when you were happy.

THE YEAR IS 1965, and the Star Ferry carries passengers between Kowloon and Hong Kong Island. Junks are moored in Aberdeen Harbour, rickshaws traverse the crowded streets, and sidewalks are filled with banana vendors. Flaccid chickens hang from butcher stands. There are no high-rises, no American department stores; laundry is pinned to clotheslines outside concrete apartment blocks; and it is, as my father liked to say, a colorful place to live.

He has lived in Hong Kong since 1962. He is the US Treasury representative—in charge of the control of foreign assets. It is a big job during a sensitive time of US relations with China. The United States has placed an embargo on trade with China. Wigs from Hong Kong can't use hair from the mainland. Chinese firecrackers, textiles, antiques, and cinnamon are not permitted to go to America. China provides Hong Kong with its water supply, a major issue for the Hilton Hotel, which is just being built. Are they allowed to use Chinese water? My father's job is to draw lines. He is thirty-seven years old, handsome, gentle, and kind. He is well liked for his low-key, unflappable manner and admired for his honesty. He is tough but fair. After graduating from Harvard Law School at the top of his class in 1952, he enlisted in the Marine Corps and served as a platoon leader. Years later when I am in college and old enough to understand the scope of this choice, I will ask why he did this and he'll explain, "I was trained in law school how to think, and I wanted to be trained how not to think." I will admire this decision and feel proud of his agile mind.

AT THE SAME time, my mother has just won a prestigious award as a promising new American poet. Her father died from a heart attack the previous year and she is using some of her inheritance to travel throughout Southeast Asia with her friend, a Chinese painter. My mother's first marriage to an Israeli violinist had been a mistake. She'd moved to Paris to live with him after Bennington College—a sudden decision that angered her father. In

Paris, she'd become friends with Anaïs Nin. Soon she would realize her husband, the volatile genius, wanted her to be a muse. They divorced. When my mother returned to New York, she established herself as an artist in her own right. Her poetry was praised and *Harper's Bazaar* listed her as one of the most beautiful and intelligent women in America. Other artists and writers became her friends—Robert Lowell, Saul Bellow, and Philip Roth. Andy Warhol made a film of her reciting her poetry. These associations greatly impress my father, as much as his powerful position, intellect, and connections with foreign journalists and diplomats in turn impress her.

They meet at a dinner party. The dinner is arranged to introduce my mother to a man who can't make it. My father is invited at the last minute, as his replacement.

THERE WAS NO one there to grab his arm and warn him, "Wait, don't go! Your life will change forever if you go to this dinner. You have no preparation for what lies ahead. You will have no resources to draw from. You will think it is one thing, but it will be something else. Your instincts are wrong. And by the time you find this out, it will be too late."

MY FATHER IS instantly struck by my mother's beauty and drawn to her vibrant manner. She is bewitching as she talks about literature, gesturing elegantly with her hands, conducting a symphony of ideas. She is glamorous, Jewish, and her wit and spirit are infectious. His dreams soar, filled with visions of their stimulating and exciting life together—practicing law and writing poetry. They find each other funny, and they are laughing. My mother's eyes shut and crease at the edges. My father's mouth opens and his teeth show. Just then my mother feels an unreasonable certainty. He will stand by her, fill up what's missing, and be a good father.

IT IS TWO days since the dinner and my mother has left Hong Kong and continued on her trip. My father is thinking about her and how she is different, creative, lively, and fun. There is a sense of concern, too; he doesn't want to miss out on an opportunity. He is, he believes, ready for marriage.

MY FATHER WAS raised in a conventional middle-class home in upstate New York with working-class Jewish immigrant parents who were happily married for fifty years. That's all he knows about marriage and why he's waited. He was the scholar of the family, skipping two grades and leaving for college at sixteen in 1945. He graduated at nineteen, knew he wanted to become a lawyer, and applied to Harvard Law and Yale. He was accepted at both but chose Harvard and deferred for a year to travel around France. He never lived in Utica after age sixteen, and he moved to Washington, DC, to work with the US Treasury Department in 1956. He felt at home when he arrived in Southeast Asia in the early sixties and remained in the Far East ever since.

My father's path and his choices were mysterious to his parents. For them, Utica was the promised land. Why would anyone want to leave? But his world expanded and there was no turning back. He is interested in poetry and literature and being in far-off, unfamiliar places. He reads my mother's book of poetry, which has just been published by Grove Press, and falls in love with a poem. It is out of character for him to make a decision impulsively, but he does. He calls her.

He asks, "Why don't you come back to Hong Kong?" There is hopeful confidence in his voice.

My mother cancels the rest of her trip, returns to Hong Kong, and stays with him at his apartment on the peak. A funicular carries the tram that ascends straight up the mountain, bringing her up up up to her savior on Mount Kellett Road. They live together for one month and six months later they are married. In three years, I will be born.

9

I t is 2002 and I am thirty-four years old. I live alone in New York City. For most of my life, I've felt under siege. Navigating. Negotiating. Taking cover.

But I can function, I can get by. I can work hard and create opportunities like this one: I have just been commissioned to write my first story for the *Sunday Times Magazine*. I have a meeting with the editor in chief, who is in town for a few days. We meet in the lobby at the Royalton Hotel on West 44th Street for a drink.

I feel at this meeting a soaring sense of hope; things will work out. It is an unfamiliar sensation, and as soon as it occurs, it is modified, tamped down with something else. Something familiar, a lot like dread.

The meeting goes well. It will lead to more work as a journalist. It will lead to living in London. It will lead to a decade of acceptable excuses that allow me to be separate from my mother. Strategies to hide. To hide is to exist.

AS I AM getting ready to leave, another writer arrives. He is older, possibly in his sixties, and joining the editor for dinner. I am introduced. "Ariel, this is . . ." I've met him before. Thirty years earlier, he'd been in my living room, at 180 East 79th Street, a guest at one of my mother's dinner parties. When I mention this, he asks who my mother is.

With trepidation, I say her name. His eyes widen. There is a look on his face that I recognize—a slight recoiling, as though taking a mental step back. This accompanies the polite, sympathetic smile.

I pretend not to notice and say good-bye. After I've left, he tells my editor, "My God. I always wondered how that little girl would survive. I thought her only choices were suicide or murder."

10

Mario is a simple man. He owns one pair of shoes. There is a bamboo cabinet with three shelves and a small area to hang clothes in. He inherited it from the previous owner of the house. "Where is all your stuff?" I asked when I first saw how he lived. "All your things?"

"That's it," he said.

He does not know about brands or authors or movie stars. He does not care. He does not feel that he is missing out. He doesn't read the newspapers.

"Do you know who that is?" I ask. It could be anyone.

"I probably did hear about that person, but it wasn't interesting to me, so I forgot. But I never forgot how to make a bowknot."

He learned how to dive when he was four, left Italy when he was twenty-one, and never lived there again. He felt stuck in the concrete and had to be in open space, near the sea.

His needs are not material. He is not a consumer and will avoid buying anything if he can. If something is old and ugly and worn-out, he doesn't see it as old and ugly and worn-out. He doesn't throw it away or replace it with something new. He will fix it with duct tape, fishing line, or rope. Supplies don't come from Home Depot.

When it comes to a computer, shirt, or kitchen utensil, he is not compelled to modernize. A flat-screen TV is "an unnecessary item." Objects are not needed for a sense of comfort. Owning books or paintings, art or ceramic vases is not important. He is calm being by the sea and in the garden. He built a fishpond and points out the Southern Cross.

IF SOMETHING IS needed, he'll make it. It would not occur to him to purchase a new toaster oven, even though the one he has is rusted and the knob has broken off. "Why?" he says when I mention this. "It does the job."

He doesn't buy things for himself, nor does he consider himself deprived. He has the same pair of sunglasses he's worn for ten years. He remembers when he bought them. It was a treat. What he says more than anything else is "No need."

I want to buy sponges. "No need," he says. There is an old piece of foam that he cuts up. I want to buy coconut water at the store and keep it in the fridge. No need. He hacks open a coconut with a machete every morning and pours the water into a recycled glass bottle. Dijon mustard is "celebrity mustard." Before I met him, he slept on the floor. A mattress is a privilege. Hot water is a luxury.

When the power goes out and the lights disappear, Mario is not disturbed. This happens frequently. The lack of light does not bother him. The lack of air-conditioning is a relief. When the Wi-Fi doesn't work, he is not in any way distressed.

"Do you know how many people live without electricity?" he asks. "We're lucky to have it at all."

. . .

HE HAS NO frame of reference for the world I came from. His childhood was peaceful; his parents were married for over forty years. He has never been to New York. Never been to America. When I met him, he asked, "What's a bagel?"

HE SHOWS ME a photo of a wooden shack. "This was my house in the Sudan," he says. He was living on a deserted island working on a pearl farm. The nearest shop was an eight-hour drive away across the desert. The island had no name; it was a lump of sand, four hundred meters by three hundred. The photo shows a square box with a roof, and in front of it an aquamarine sea. He had a generator and a filter that turned salt water into drinking water. No neighbors; food was delivered once a week. He lived on this island for four months.

"When was this?" I ask.

He tells me it was ten years earlier.

This is when I was living in West London and working full-time as a journalist for the *Sunday Times*.

IN 1997, MARIO worked on a boat in Sumatra. He was doing a sand survey. There wasn't much to do and the others on the boat were Japanese, Chinese, Filipino, and Malaysian. They spoke English, but he didn't interact with them. He closed himself off and made drawings. For one month he didn't say a single word. Not even to hear the sound of his voice? I asked this in disbelief. He said no. Not a word.

"I didn't need to talk to anybody and nobody needed to talk to me."

I think about this often. That silence, for him, is conversation.

WHEN WE HAVE fish for dinner, he will go into the ocean with his spear gun, free-diving and holding his breath for several minutes while he hides on the sea bed in the reef. He shoots the fish, guts it, and cooks it.

"Is that snapper?" I ask when I see it in the pan.

He sighs. "No, that's a jackfish."

This is the same sigh I give when he asks, "What's the *New York Times*?"

We don't hold it against each other. When I show him an article I wrote, he says, "So many words!" and I laugh because of how different we are.

I ASK MARIO, "Could you be happy with a wordless life?"

"Very happy," he says.

"Not me," I state.

"No kidding."

I continue, "So if you could be happy with a wordless life and that's the opposite of what I want, what does that mean?"

He pauses for a second and says, "That we make a good balance."

I TOLD HIM there is a place in America called the Container Store. The look on his face was astonishment. He couldn't believe such a place existed. His taste is basic. He is, in many ways, like a local Balinese person. He identifies with those who are less fortunate and sees himself as lucky. He is satisfied with what he has and does not seek more. He does not have to work to be in the moment with affirmations or discipline; it is his natural state.

Every day for sixteen years he has gone to the same beach, to the same job, and enjoys it. "It is not the same job," he says. "Because one day I teach diving, one day I teach kitesurfing, one day I teach surfing." He is at home in the water. He is content.

WHAT WE HAVE in common are values. There is stability. There is loyalty. He is decent and undemanding. His character is solid. He could never manipulate. He wouldn't know how. He doesn't pretend to be anyone he's not and he can spot a phony. He doesn't ask people questions he doesn't care about the answers to. And what people think of him is irrelevant. He won't say "Nice to see you again!" if he doesn't feel it. He's got nothing to prove. His pleasures in life are not from things. The beauty he sees is in nature.

What he is interested in is how to build a tree house. Or how to place the stone tiles in the garden in order to change the path. He is focused on things that improve his life in a practical way.

The curiosity he has is in different areas. During the rainy season when the winged termites come out in droves at dusk, they are drawn to the light. He wondered what they would taste like. He caught a few dozen, boiled them in a pot, and ate them. The girls and I declined. "They taste like sweet corn," he said.

MARIO HAS AN answer for everything and is often bemused with my discomfort.

"There's a giant rat in the kitchen," I say.

He responds in his gentle tone. "We live in the country, *amore*."

"What happens if the spitting cobra spits in my eyes?" I ask.

"You will go blind. Wear your glasses."

I miss having a living room.

"The garden is our living room," he says.

To avoid getting drenched during the rainy season, I

carry an umbrella going from the kitchen to our bungalow.

"*Amore!*" He smiles. "It's raining in the living room."

HIS TRADITIONAL BALINESE property has four small bungalows with a garden in the center and a separate, open
kitchen. When I moved in, guests and friends occupied
the bungalows, and there were constant people roaming
around. The kitchen is largely outdoors and shared. In
the morning, there were strangers, often speaking another
language, making themselves coffee. Mario lived in one
of the bungalows. He enjoyed having people around. But
I was not used to this. Strangers would drop by, unannounced. When I came back to the house, there was no
way to know who would be there. I would come home to
visitors talking in German. Changes were made so that I
could have privacy. So that I could have refuge.

WHAT CONNECTS US are the basics, tenets of normalcy I
never had. Need is redefined. Pots and pans, knives and
dish towels, bed linens and bath mats don't have to match.
They don't have to even exist.

11

I grew up on the Upper East Side of Manhattan, in a prewar building. 180 East 79th Street, between Lexington and Third. Penthouse G. My mother purchased the apartment in 1967, the year before I was born, with the inheritance she received from her father. It was an unconventional setting filled with books and artifacts, sunlight and photographs. The apartment was decorated with people. Artists, writers, musicians, belly dancers. When a Chinese painter came for a visit, he'd drawn a charcoal mural on the living room wall by the time he left. In the kitchen there were books. In my mother's bedroom there were bowls. Her taste reflected a cultured aesthetic, original and sophisticated; everything had a story. Things—some that were worth money, some that weren't—were never for the sake of making a statement. They were there because they had meaning. And she saw their beauty because of this. There were fresh calla lilies on the coffee table. Amlash terra-cotta pottery from Persia in the living room. Books on every flat surface. And photos of my mother—with Henry Miller; with Gloria Steinem; with Donald, her boyfriend; with my father; with me. Happy times. Scotch-taped to the wall. Or punctured with thumbtacks. Life in a topsy-turvy spectacle, a Fellini-like universe with a view from the terrace.

12

After Kiki died there was a year of nannies moving in and moving out, taking care of me. None of them stayed longer than a few months. A nanny would come to live with us for a while, in the spare room off the kitchen, until she realized the pay was not worth the aggravation. There was Nadej. There was Jeanie. There was, "I forgot her name." And others. When it came time for the departure, they would sneak away. Or there would be an explosion. My mother would withhold their paycheck and say they didn't deserve it. But they would leave anyway. Departing the same day, wearing their uniform. Cursing in Polish or Portuguese, desperate to get out.

WHEN JOSEPHINE ARRIVED, I knew better then to get attached. But she was different from the others. She was from Belgium and expressed, without hesitation, her opinions on how things should be done. She would wear what she wanted. Dinner would be at five-thirty. She would scold my mother because I had no set times for meals or for bed. "This child," she said, shaking her head, "needs discipline." She took control.

My Dear Harvey,

I have just spent 2 hours at 180. When I arrived the new nurse (Josephine) met me. Suzanne was in bed and Ariel, in her nightgown, was sitting on the floor playing alone with her toys. I've yet to go there and not find her in her room alone. Josephine was afraid to tell me what was going on because Suzanne would fire her. "Ariel bosses me around all the time," Josie said. "And when I try to make Ariel behave, the Mrs. yells at me. Ariel is such a difficult child." No, I said. "She isn't. She wasn't always like this."

xo Rita

RITA MET MY father in 1970 when he was going through the divorce from my mother and staying at the Harvard Club. One night a friend of my father's had a party and Rita was there. She too was recently divorced.

Rita worked at *The Saturday Evening Post* as an editor, and during the time she was dating my father, she helped start *Ms.* magazine with Gloria Steinem. Rita was warm, cheerful, affectionate, and silly. She was the fairy godmother who fixed what was broken and filled in the cracks. With attention, with care, with words that were never wasted. I could count on what Rita said.

. . .

RITA AND MY father were together for two years, and in early 1972, after he moved away, she remained close to us both. She made a point of staying in my life. She came over to the apartment to spend time with me and we sat, just the two of us, on the floor of my bedroom and wore Mickey Mouse ears and spent hours playing Candy Land and Chutes and Ladders while my mother stayed in her bedroom or entertained during one of her parties.

Rita and I went to the zoo in Central Park. Afterward we rolled around on the Great Lawn and she didn't mind grass stains or dirt or mud and we stayed out all day, practicing handstands and cartwheels with her spotting me. She was such a caring person that my mother encouraged her to spend as much time with me as she could.

When the doorman announced Rita was on the way up, I stood in the foyer to wait. The elevator doors opened and I jumped up into her arms.

"Hello, Monkey," she'd say. "I missed you."

I looked forward to her visits; she was the only person, aside from my father and Josie, that I let hug me.

Even though my mother welcomed Rita's presence, she was threatened by it as well. She sometimes snapped, "Well, if you love Rita so much, go live with her!"

But I knew that hours or maybe minutes later, she'd come around. Because if someone could give me things that she couldn't, such as time or attention, she wouldn't deny me their company. She would allow it. And later resent it.

· · ·

ONE MORNING I woke up inconsolable. My mother called Rita. "None of us can calm her down," she said. It was seven-thirty. "She wants to talk to you. Will you speak to her?"

"Of course," Rita replied. "What do you think the problem is?"

"She misses you. She keeps crying for you."

Rita got on the phone, but I was sobbing so hard, I couldn't speak. She calmed me down and told a story about when we played in the park on the statue of Alice in Wonderland. Soon she realized that I didn't want to go to school if I thought I could be with her. My mother snatched the receiver from my hand.

"Rita, you have to see Ariel more." It was a demand. I sat on the bed next to my mother and listened as she shouted into the phone. "Why is it so hard for you to understand that a child can love and have feelings? She loves you, and if you don't understand that, then I really pity you."

I tugged at my mother's robe. "Don't yell at her, please— don't upset her."

She continued. "It's normal for Ariel to feel like this. She's a very sad and lonely child. It's hard for her not having two parents. First her father left, then Kiki died. You've got to see her. Don't be like her father and pretend you're too busy."

Half an hour later, she called Rita back.

"Don't worry," my mother said. "Ariel is no longer hysterical and everything is fine."

.   .   .

THE FIRST TIME Rita met my mother, she was nervous. It was 1973 and the documentary my mother made on the women's movement was opening at a cinema on Fifth Avenue. *Ms.* magazine gave out passes to the event, and Rita decided to go with a colleague. When she arrived at the theater, a group of feminists out in front were holding a banner and singing anthems. "Move on over, or we'll move on over you!" Photographers were covering the scene. Reporters had shown up. Bystanders had gathered and were staring at the assembly of radical women. Front and center was Florynce Kennedy— fierce and outspoken and wearing her leather cowboy hat, middle "fuck you" finger high in the air. My mother was beside Flo, causing a sensation. Being a troublemaker was energizing. It excited her. She relished the spectacle.

"This was not surprising," Rita wrote in her letter to my father. "But what did surprise me was that Ariel was in her mother's arms, singing loudly and proclaiming her liberation."

My mother stood near the entrance to the theater, greeting people. "Hurry up, this kid's getting heavy," she said to no one in particular.

A few seconds later, I spotted Rita. "Mommy, look who's here!" I said, leaning toward her. My mother had spoken with her on the phone, but they'd never met in person. She immediately passed me into Rita's arms.

"Oh, are you her teacher?" she asked.

"No, I'm Ariel's friend, Rita," she replied, dismayed that my mother didn't know who my teachers were.

My mother asked Rita to take me for a while because she was so busy. Rita and I stood on the sidelines catching up. She bent down and I sat on her knee.

"Did you know that Kiki went to heaven?" I asked.

"Yes," Rita said. "And while Kiki is very happy there, we feel a little sad because we miss her."

I nodded and played with her hair. I tugged at her braids. We continued chatting as strangers from my mother's dinner parties came over to kiss me hello. I was bewildered by all the commotion, and each time it happened, I hugged Rita tighter.

We moved back to where the action was. I located my mother and told her I had to use the bathroom.

"Do you want to go with me or with Aunt Rita?" she asked. She had known Rita for five minutes.

WE FOUND OUR way to the bathroom and then to our seats. I sat on Rita's lap for the entire two hours. My mother was on-camera most of the time and the film was told with her voice-over and filled with her poetry. In one scene she wears a papier-mâché crocodile mask over her head. She comments on the spectacle as masquerade. As she and Flo confront the media at the 1972 Democratic National Convention, she is the zany heroine.

She sneaks into the convention hall with Liz Renay, a six-foot-tall blond stripper in a revealing sequined dress, determined and defiant. And as the men predictably respond with all eyes on breasts, my mother later comments from a beach chair, "If a man walked into a convention with a huge cock, would women rush up and ask, 'Who is he, where is he, what's his name?'"

THERE IS A tongue-in-cheek element to her belligerence. The poet as crusader can get away with anything. The more outrageous, the better. If the media makes women out to be freaks, why not *be* a freak? she asks. As she verbally challenges the journalist Mike Wallace, who stares back at her with a glazed look on his face, as though he is staring at an alien, in her voice-over she confesses, "I've never had so much fun as when I make trouble."

IN ONE SEQUENCE, my mother and Flo are talking about motherhood. Flo says it isn't children that imprison women, but motherhood itself. My mother claims that no one wants to spend time with a dull, babbling two-year-old.

I turned to Rita and said, "I'm glad I'm not two."

When the film is over, my mother asked Rita if she would take me home and then come to the after party, and when Rita told her no, my mother insisted.

"Oh, but you can stay for an hour, at least."

"I was happy to have had time with Ariel," Rita later

wrote to my father. "And it wasn't until I got home that I wondered how Suzanne could have so freely left her daughter with a perfect stranger. I took care of her and loved every second of it, but how could she know that? And she wanted me to take her home? I give up."

But she didn't give up.

The letter to my father ends with these words: "No matter how carried away I may get about the politics of the world, the status of women or personal problems, it takes a simple one-on-one visit with your dear little girl to readjust my sense of values. The next time Suzanne asks me to take Ariel I just may kidnap her. Sometimes I'm crazy enough to think I could get away with it . . . but don't worry, I won't try."

MY MOTHER OFTEN had fund-raisers for the women's movement in our living room, and there were lots of women with floppy hats and raised voices. Flo didn't alter her combative attitude when she spoke to me. In her hot-pink sunglasses she found someone equally untamed and ferocious in my mother. "Your mother is one tough motherfucker. Right, baby?" she'd ask. She handed me a cigarette when I was five to take a puff.

WHEN I LOOK at this film as an adult, I admire my mother's willingness to defy convention. There is a scene where she is tap-dancing on the pavement in front of the White House. I see her joyfulness. I see a campaigner. On behalf of women. On behalf of herself. When she had a cause, she was fanatical. Lack of boundaries was an asset. Her megaphone was always on.

But I see the absurdity, too. Because heartfelt feminist beliefs were trumped by emotional needs. Clinging to men, begging them not to abandon her. Cries of "I need you, don't leave me." My witnessing contradictions play out in everyday life was routine. And in the absence of consistency, admiration unravels.

IT IS NEARLY Christmas, I am six years old, and Rita has come to visit after work. My mother has purchased a Christmas tree. When Rita arrives, I am trimming the tree with my mother and Josie. My mother's mood is upbeat. She suggests Rita stay for dinner.

The trimming is continually interrupted because my mother takes phone calls in the other room. When she returns, I become angry with her, and she says, "You know, Ariel, most people trim the tree when the children are in bed. And now I know why."

She invites Rita to attend the Christmas Eve party she is having. "It begins at midnight," she says. "Ariel is hosting."

When Rita declines, my mother asks her to spend Christmas Day with us instead. Rita explains she has plans with her family, but my mother doesn't consider this an obstacle.

"Oh, but couldn't you come for a while? Ariel would love that."

After that, my mother takes another phone call in her bedroom, and when she emerges, she is wearing a long gown, with her fur coat over her arm.

"Mommy, you promised to have dinner with me!" I scream.

"I promised to sit at the table with you, and I will. For a few minutes. Then you and Rita and Josie can have dinner together. Isn't that what you wanted?"

We move to the dining room, and I have made place cards for my mother and Rita and Josie. Each table setting has a crystal ball ornament with everyone's favorite color.

My mother sits with us and has a glass of wine. As Josie brings out the hamburgers, my mother gets up to leave. I become upset because my mother had promised to put me to bed. "Rita, will you stay with me?" I ask.

She agrees and I feel soothed.

Rita comes with me to my bedroom, and she sees three letters from my father on the table. Unopened. The procedure is usually that Josie reads these letters to me after dinner while my mother is with guests or out for the evening. Josie has come in the room to prepare me for bed. "This evening when we got back from Ariel's psychiatrist," she explains, "the missus wanted to trim the tree. Mr. Harvey writes beautiful letters. I will read them to her tomorrow."

I ask Rita to wait until I fall asleep.

"Before you leave, will you turn the lights off the tree?" I am worried about a fire. Rita sits on the edge of the bed and tucks me in. As she gets up to leave, I keep calling for her to come back for more hugs.

SHE LEAVES MY bedroom and goes to the kitchen to help Josie clean up.

"The missus has spent more time with Ariel tonight than she has the whole time I've been here," Josie says.

"Why do you suppose that is?" Rita asks.

"Because you're here. And she's afraid you will write to Ariel's father about what you see. She was so loving tonight. Ach, it's an act."

Josie had been there only a few months. Rita was new to my mother's behavior. They hadn't yet accepted how powerless they were. But they stayed. Even though they were torn. They stayed.

13

I relied on Josie for everything. She would never leave me. She was dependable. She woke me up in the mornings and put me to bed. She walked me to school, and at the end of the day, she stood there waiting to pick me up. She took me to the dentist and sat in the waiting room, knitting chunky woolen vests, until the appointment was over. She took me to my piano lesson and sat in Central Park until I was through. She helped with my homework, braided my hair, cooked and ate all of my meals with me. Every morning and every night. She had one day off a week, and during that day I stayed in my room reading or drawing.

When my mother demanded that Josie work through her day off, they argued. Josie would shout at my mother and say she needed a rest. Then my mother would fire her. This happened whenever Josie stood up to her. It could occur at any minute over anything. I asked my mother, "Will Josie be here when I wake up?" and she would snap, "No," calling her a traitor. I would start to cry and beg her not to fire Josie until she promised she wouldn't. But she would anyway. There would be arguments because Josie didn't approve of my mother's bad habits—walking around naked, having sex with the boyfriend who gave her a black eye and letting him sleep over, dropping cigarette butts into the coffee mug, letting the bathtub overflow, entertaining on school nights; it was a long list.

JOSEPHINE HAD NEVER been married, never had children, and was several years older than my mother. She was sturdy, with a winsome smile and freckled skin that made her seem maternal. She wore her auburn hair in a bun that made her seem taller than her five-foot-two frame. She called it a topknot.

Eventually I began to trust her and we developed a bond. As I got older, one of the most hurtful things I could say to my mother was "You didn't raise me. Josie did." My mother would point out that she was the one who paid Josie to take care of me. Then she'd accuse Josie of turning me against her. Just as my father did.

JOSIE WOULD MAKE dinner for us every night and we would sit down to eat at five-thirty. The time never changed. It was part of the structure. My mother always insisted there be a place set for her—she wanted to be included—but then she wouldn't show up. We'd eat dinner with a place mat and napkin set in front of an empty chair.

I would go to my mother's room and let her know dinner was ready. "I'll be right there," she'd say. Time passed. After her phone calls ended, my mother would make an appearance.

"You don't promise a child you'll show up and then not make it," Josie would say. "Ariel has been waiting for you."

My mother insisted that I didn't mind. "Do you?"

She'd look right at me. I had to lie.

JOSIE SAYS, "THERE'S shit in the bed."

I don't ask why there's shit in the bed.

She is aggressively pulling the sheets off the mattress in my mother's bedroom and throwing them on the floor. "Why should I have to put up with this?" She is not expecting me to answer her. It was as though I wasn't there.

I am there. I am standing in the doorway looking on.

"Why do you think no one else will stay in this job? No one else will put up with her. Why should I have to? I'm not a maid."

I panic. "You're not going to leave, are you?"

She doesn't answer me.

MY MOTHER HAD accidents. That's what they were called. Peeing in her pants was a frequent accident. "Give me a second," she would announce when she arrived home and I went to the door to greet her. "I've had an accident." There was no shame in this announcement.

Sometimes she would come home and be in such a rush

to make a phone call, I would see her standing in the kitchen, receiver to her ear, with one leg tightly crossed over the other so as to prevent the pee from coming out. She would hold this pose for a few seconds and concentrate on not wetting herself.

She would make the *shhh* gesture, furrow her brow, and press her finger to her mouth until she was ready to talk to me. When she hung up the phone, I would ask her to change out of her soggy sweatpants.

"I'm about to," she'd say. "I haven't had time."

I watch as she moves past me, inching forward, sashaying in an almost elegant manner, her arms swaying as one leg sharply crisscrosses the other with precise timing so that there is no open space between her legs.

"It's not my fault," she calls out. "I have a bladder problem."

INSTRUCTING MY MOTHER on manners or etiquette or on how to behave elicited amused disapproval. "No bringing up mommy," she'd say. I told her: Please don't blow your nose into your T-shirt. Or into the linen napkin at a restaurant. Someone else has to take that away. Are you wearing underwear? Can you brush your hair? Your nightgown is inside out. Please don't wear it to Parents' Day. Did you say thank you? Don't do that. Don't say that.

She would snap, "How did you become so conventional?"

· · ·

THERE WERE NO barriers between what my mother was experiencing and what I was exposed to. "We don't keep secrets from each other" was a commandment. Nothing was ever withheld.

MY MOTHER HAS a new lover. She has been shouting into the telephone in the kitchen and he must have hung up on her because as she strides through the living room, her light pink ruffled bathrobe untied at the waist so that it looks like a cape flowing behind her naked body, she is in a state. She blurts out, "I miss screwing him. Where are the matches?"

I am sitting on the sofa. "By the stove where they always are."

She gives me a quick glance. "Can you help me, please?" She is frantic. "I need a light for my cigarette."

He had a huge cock. That's what she is telling me about her boyfriend. I am not old enough to be hearing this information. Discomfort races through my body.

I follow her into the kitchen. "Where are the fucking matches?" she cries out. She is opening drawers and cabinets in an agitated manner.

The Spaniard had wide shoulders and wore expensive suits. He smelled of cologne. He was married. He drank a lot. When she was happy with him, all was right in the world. She ended up in the hospital after they argued. She lent him money. Gave him money. He swindled her out of the money. He was a freeloader. A hustler. A thief. "He stole ten thousand dollars and I want him arrested!" She called the police. This was the story. He never loved her. He used her. She threatened to have his green card revoked.

DAYS LATER, WHEN I ask her not to use the word *cock*, she tells me that the word is vulgar and she doesn't use it.

THE FIRST TIME I heard the term *gaslighting*, I was in my late thirties. I was walking with a friend on West 27th Street in Manhattan. It was nighttime, after dinner, and he was finishing a story about a woman he was no longer involved with. A woman who had made him doubt his perception of reality. He was describing an argument they'd had.

"And then I said"—his voice became a roar of indignation—"don't you *gaslight* me!"

He hissed the rebellion into the air. I didn't respond and we continued walking, neither of us making a comment to the other but reflecting privately on our experience as veterans of a psychological ambush. I'd never met that word before, but it wasn't a stranger.

Our paths had crossed. The encounter wasn't a surprise. Our meeting was more like confirmation. Yes, I know you. There's a name for that. There's a term for that.

JOSIE COULD BE like a martinet. She was in charge and she was strict. So strict that her beating me with a hanger or a hairbrush was not unusual. How many times did she have to tell me to do my homework? I talked back to her when she tried to discipline me. She spanked me so hard that her hand would swell and become red and she'd have to stop. She would chase me around the dining room table waving a wire hanger in the air until I was trapped in a corner, unable to get away. I promised I would listen to her; I would do what she wanted and not misbehave.

"I can't take it!" she shouted. She looked so disheartened. I was afraid that she'd given up on me.

My mother would become furious with her for hitting me. She was protective. But then she'd hit me as well. Or she'd throw things, usually a shoe. But she had terrible aim and I laughed at her when she missed, which only made it worse.

But when Josie made up her mind that she couldn't control me and had no choice but to quit, this was the worst punishment of all. I would apologize for not listening to her and beg my mother not to let Josie leave. My mother would plead with Josie to stay. "How can you do this to Ariel? If you leave, it will damage her even more."

DURING THE DAY I would worry that when Josie came to pick me up at school she would inform me that my mother had fired her while I'd been gone. Or worse, I worried that my mother *had* fired her and would send someone I'd never met to pick me up. I'd get out of school at the exit on 75th Street between Park and Madison and there would be a stranger waiting for me. Linda was waiting. Linda who? The woman my mother had met at the dry cleaner's or in the elevator or at the beauty parlor, someone who was investing in her musical. I'd get home to find Josie packing her suitcases, dabbing her bloodshot eyes with a tissue. She would tell me she couldn't take it anymore and that she was getting an ulcer.

I CRIED THAT my mother didn't mean what she said and begged her please not to go. I sat on the step stool in the kitchen near the stove and watched as she packed up her room. She threw items into her suitcase—hand-knit vests and rosary beads. Sometimes while she was packing my mother would return, enraged. She would grab Josie's arm to prevent her from leaving. "You're not going anywhere!"

My mother would plant herself firmly in front of the door, pushing Josie away if she tried to get past. The two of them would tussle—Josie trying to shove my mother out of the way, my mother refusing to let her go. They would have a tug-of-war over the suitcase that would escalate into a violent scene, and I would implore Josie not to leave out of fear she'd be physically harmed if she continued to try. I would insert myself in the middle and urge them to stop.

Josie would say that she loved me, but she had her health to think of. The ulcer was getting worse. So a few hours later, after my mother calmed down and retired to her bedroom at the opposite end of the apartment, I'd help Josie sneak out. Ringing the bell for the service elevator, then guarding the kitchen door, I'd be the lookout to make sure my mother couldn't accost her.

AFTER JOSIE LEFT, my mother announced she'd take care of me herself. A few hours later she'd be on the phone with the employment agency pleading with them to send someone over as soon as possible. She couldn't cope. The employment agency refused to send a new person to be interviewed. They didn't care how much she paid; they didn't want anyone else to be attacked. When my mother hung up, she started to cry. She felt persecuted.

WHEN SOMEBODY NEW arrived, I wanted to explain how it worked. I wanted to explain that there would be days when my mother was kind and generous, giving her presents such as orchids and poems by Pablo Neruda and Federico García Lorca. She would treat the new person like a friend, take her into her confidence, and ask her for advice; these were the days to expect to feel special. But then there would be other days. When my mother would have an accident and not make it to the bathroom in time. Or there would be nights when dishes would be broken in a drunken fight and pieces remained on the dining room floor, waiting to be swept away. I wanted to explain to this stranger who had come to live with us that when my mother yelled, she didn't mean what she said, or when she walked around naked, not to be frightened, not to leave, it would all be okay, she would recover, it would pass. And that a day or an hour later, it would be forgotten.

As soon as the new person became the old person, my mother began making daily phone calls to Josie at her new employer's. She offered kind words, more money, more days off, paid vacations; she promised to behave, anything to get her to come back.

Dear Harvey,

The other evening I went over to 180 after a call from Ariel. There was a woman named Maria there. She was the third housekeeper now that Josie has left again. I sat with Ariel and we did her homework.

The following morning at 7:30 Ariel called me. These early-morning calls are generally from a very sad little girl and this was no exception. We planned to spend the afternoon together. Maria had, of course, now left. We didn't talk much about that. Each time someone leaves, Ariel just says, "She's not here anymore."

xo Rita

WHEN I RETURNED from one summer with my father in Thailand, I discovered Josie was no longer at 180. She was there when I left; when I got home, she was gone.

Within two hours of my arriving back at the apartment, my mother called Rita.

"Ariel has just returned from Bangkok and she would love to see you. She is very sad that Josie has left her."

My mother put me on the phone.

My voice was small and sleepy. I asked Rita to come for a visit.

"Have you met the new person who takes care of me?" I asked.

AFTER THAT, I went to sleep to recover from the jet lag, and when I woke up, Rita was seated on the edge of my bed. She read me a story, and as she started to leave, I made a cage with my arms around her so that she couldn't get out. I told her my mother was planning a big party and that I was worried about the noise.

"I'm afraid I won't get any rest," I said.

A FEW WEEKS passed. Rita arrived at 180, and I was once again asleep. My mother was in a housedress and Ina (the new person) was preparing lunch for my mother and a guest. Rita entered my room, woke me up, and told me to get dressed so that we could go out. She had planned a visit to the Hayden Planetarium.

"Look, Rita," I said, "my fish has died."

The water in the fishbowl was filthy and the fish had been dead for some time. My mother came in the room, looked at the fish, and clutched her stomach as if she was about to be sick. Rita asked her to take me out of the room and said she would get rid of the fish. "Oh, thank you," my mother said. "I don't know what I would have done."

Rita took care of this simple task, flushing the fish down the toilet. She cleaned the bowl, too. Then she helped me get dressed while my mother took a phone call and her guest roamed around the apartment.

Rita had pigtails in her hair. "I want some, too!" I said. I inform her that I haven't washed my hair in two weeks or taken a bath in a week. Rita later writes to my father, "It sure looked like it."

After lunch, Rita took me on the 79th Street cross-town bus to the planetarium. She wrote to my father: "It was grand. Ariel scampered around asking more questions than I was able to answer. It was a beautiful afternoon."

When we returned to 180 at five-thirty in the afternoon, there were people having drinks in the living room and Ina was not around. Reluctant to leave me on my own, Rita made sure I had dinner and a bath. Before leaving, she put me to bed.

WITH JOSIE GONE, I was sent for a visit with my father's mother in upstate New York. When I got back, my mother called Rita. She told her she was going to Chicago for the weekend and wanted to make sure Rita could spend time with me.

"I've got a new maid for her, but she loves to see you," my mother said.

She put me on the phone.

"I am going to Scarsdale tonight," I said. This is where my mother's mother lives. "I go from one grandmother to the other."

When Rita arrived for the weekend, my mother's plans had changed. She was not in Chicago. She was in her bedroom. Rita walked into my room and was surprised to see Josie there visiting with me.

"Josie has agreed to come back," I said. I was excited about this.

·   ·   ·

LATER THAT EVENING, Josie called Rita and explained why she was returning. My mother had been putting pressure on her, and finally she had said yes. Josie told her, "She promised no more parties on weeknights; I would have time off each week and get four weeks paid vacation." Rita doesn't believe my mother will keep her word.

"If she breaks the promise," Josie said, "I'll just pack up and leave. She knows now that I'll do it."

> *Dear Harvey,*
>
> *By now you've probably heard that Josie is returning to 180. While it's true that Josie has a very strong self-interest, she will take good care of Ariel. She will get her to school on time, see that she does her homework and will make sure that she's clean and keep her well-fed. Those have got to be considered plusses.*
> *When Ariel is alone with me, or alone with people she trusts, she is a gem. A happy little girl. There is no problem. But Josie knows that Ariel doesn't have full faith in her anymore. Josie said, "Ariel knows her mother spent thousands of dollars to get me back. New dishwasher, redecorating my room, full paid vacation in cash. She says I can't really love her if I had to be bought back."*

I KNEW JOSIE was not fully on my side. I knew, at seven years old, that her allegiance was compromised. She would not have returned if it hadn't been to her financial benefit. It was a job. I was a job. To put up with my mother, it had to be worth it.

THE FIRST NIGHT Josie moved back into her room, I climbed into her bed and slept next to her. I asked her to promise never to leave me again. But she told me she couldn't promise me that. She had to wait and see if my mother "shaped up."

For a few weeks after Josie returned, my mother stayed on her best behavior. She was a changed person. Only it didn't last. Josie got fired again or quit, and this went on for the entire twelve years that she was with us.

14

Surf. Wake. Kite. Wind. These are the words on the flag that flies outside where Mario works. I am sitting on a wooden stool. Bright-colored photos of wakeboarding and kitesurfing action shots adorn the wall. Surfer girls in bikinis. Tan bodies in board shorts. T-shirts and sunglasses and beers are for sale. The view is of the beach. Life is easy. No stress. The talk is of wind and knots and weather conditions. It never gets old. The mood is upbeat. Reggae music is playing. The white surf at the reef breaks. The sun shines.

THE GIRLS ARE running toward me. They are wearing their one-piece Speedo swimsuits and they shout, "Ariel!" in unison because they have just spotted me and they are happy to see me. They are smiling, with wide gaps where their two front teeth used to be. It is late afternoon and they have been there all day, playing on their own. I haven't seen them for a few hours.

"I missed you!" one of them says as her arms wrap around my waist.

"I missed you, too." I respond without hesitation.

"Will you come swimming with us?" Her eyes are expectant.

.   .   .

WE PLAY IN the ocean. The tide is low and I crouch down on my haunches so that my shoulders are underwater and my feet are flat on the sand. I pretend to be a turtle and they take turns riding on my back. We float for a while and then we are mermaids splashing around. Our hair is tangled in seaweed. Small waves wash over us and the salty water gets in our mouths; we spit it up into the air in an arc. Then we dive beneath the surface and burst up again, like dolphins.

I NEVER WANTED to be a mother. When friends would speak about their desire to have a baby, I realized that I didn't share this feeling. I didn't crave it or need it or feel that my life would be incomplete without it. There was never a fear that I would miss out.

I was not against having a child, but I wasn't seeking it either. What I had instead was ambivalence. And this ambivalence was so muted that it wasn't even acknowledged or explored. It just existed in me like a virus that was asymptomatic.

HOWEVER, MY AMBIVALENCE was silently guiding my decisions and choices. Because if I had felt compelled to have a child, I might have been galvanized into doing all sorts of things I didn't do. I would have had to take inventory, to examine my options and determine what I wanted. Did I want a family? Could I have a family? Were having these connections in my life important? These were questions I didn't ask myself. Wanting to love and be loved didn't assume a specific shape or form.

I didn't dream about specifics. Marriage or children— there was no blueprint for that. One day I wouldn't feel trapped. That was the aspiration. Other than that, adulthood was an empty road.

IF I'D THOUGHT about specifics, I would have been forced to scrutinize decisions in a way that accounted for the biological reality. Instead, I indulged in procrastination, an indulgence of deferment. It was a carelessness that didn't require alcohol or drugs, because altering reality with substances wasn't a temptation. Reality had been altered enough.

TURNING FORTY FELT the same as turning thirty or twenty. The goals others had for chronological or material milestones were irrelevant to me. Interior goals took precedence. Where did I want to be at forty? I wanted not to feel stuck.

I didn't know how to get there. I had no fear about getting older because I lived in an arrested state, where there was only a floating timelessness.

·

I WAS WEARING red lipstick, high heels, and a black dress that my friend Laura had endorsed. We'd gone shopping together weeks earlier in New York when I found out I'd been nominated for the award. "We have to find you a dress!" she'd exclaimed, and I wished I shared her enthusiasm. I stood barefoot outside the dressing room, wearing a fifties-style prom dress after having modeled half a dozen different options for her approval. "I'll get this one," I said. "It's fine."

"Aren't you excited?" she asked. I shrugged. I wanted it over with.

The night of the British Press Awards I got dressed alone in my flat in London. I looked forward to returning, taking off the makeup, getting into my pajamas, making a cup of tea, and going to sleep. At thirty-eight years old, I should have been. I should have been happy. I should have been proud. I'd done good work and it had been recognized. I was living in broad strokes and headlines. It was an autopilot existence.

"I don't want to be here," I said. That was my greeting to him when we ran into each other in the lobby on our way in. He'd arrived separately.

He smiled. "Well, you look lovely."

We couldn't be seen together as a couple. It was a public event and assumptions would be made that would be accurate and it would cause trouble for him, for me, for us. From the beginning he had told me we had no future. That I couldn't expect more—and I accepted that. But not really. Our life was a secret. I was a secret. And because of this, there was no advancing forward. More didn't feel realistic.

It was enough that I had devotion, attention, time, and care. And episodic joy.

The ceremony was about to begin and we would be in the same room, at separate tables. He wasn't one to accept defeat, and as we stood lingering for a few moments surrounded by colleagues, he tried to lift my spirits. "Cheer up, sweetheart," he said. "It's gonna be your night."

"What does that mean?" I asked. I could say anything to him, and often did. How could it be my night when I couldn't hold his hand?

I sat at the *Sunday Times* table, a place card with my name on it in front of my poached salmon. He sat on the other side of the room, but if I tilted my head to the left and squinted past hairdos and tuxedoed shoulders, I could spot him. Whenever I did this, he would spot me, too. We would stare at each other for a few seconds and silently share the experience. Solitary confinement, with company.

The night went on. My name was called. Infinite possibility was by my side, a dozen tables away. I was holding hands with him as I walked to the podium, invisibly connected to his intelligence and strength.

As I was being congratulated, I could move through it all and participate. But there was always somewhere else I wanted to be. Only that place didn't exist.

MY MOTHER SAYS, "Don't let work be your whole life or you'll miss out on having a child."

When she says this, I feel as though I am drowning.

She reminds me, "You need to have balance. The way I had."

DEADLINES FOR PERSONAL choices weren't overlooked. They weren't postponed. They were nonexistent. They must have been. Or I would have considered the outcome before making that phone call. Before responding to that email that I should have ignored. Before saying yes when I should have said no. Seemingly inconsequential actions with predictable outcomes. Actions that added up and left me in a holding pattern. Hovering above the runway of trust without ever having to land.

MY MOTHER SAYS, "I hope one day you will have a child of your own so that you can understand the pain I go through."

If I wanted a sleepover at a friend's house, it was a mission.

"You know I don't want to be alone," she tells me. "You can have her sleep over here."

The negotiation began. "But it's a slumber party. All my friends will be there."

She tells me to stop whining.

"Invite them here."

She explains that I should be grateful to have a mother who loves me. "Or would you prefer I don't care? You're lucky you have an attentive mother who wants you around."

"WHO DO YOU love more?" my mother asks, stepping out of the tub, with suds clinging to her belly. "Your daddy or me?"

I say, "Don't ask me that. I can't choose."

But she didn't listen and as she toweled herself off and powderpuffed her naked body, she asked it again until I gave her the answer she wanted to hear.

"You," I say.

Loving anyone more than her would have been a betrayal.

IF I WANTED independence in any way, I was hurting her. Her feeling that she was being abandoned would trigger her aggression. Her behavior threatened my safety. I deserved it. I was out to get her. I'd been poisoned against her. I wasn't smart enough to get it. I wasn't appreciative of who she was and what she did. I was special, brilliant, and talented. All she cared about was my happiness. I love you meant nothing. I hate you meant nothing. She meant all of it. I felt none of it.

By the time I finally grew up, I was exhausted.

.   .   .

I WAS FORTY-FOUR years old and having dinner with a friend one evening in a Greek restaurant when she said, "The role of a parent is to prepare the child and give them tools to go off in life and expect nothing in return." I sat there. I reached for my notebook. "Can you say that again?" I asked. The words were liquid mercury spilling off the table. I couldn't grasp them.

Sometimes the invisible failures are not understood until it's too late. And what prevails is the sense of unavoidable destiny. Standing in the pit of a crevasse, with a rope to safety just inches away and out of reach. If only I was half an inch taller. There is always that wish for the impossible. For the sick parent to recover, the impulsive parent to have self-control, the unpredictable parent to be consistent, the irrational parent to respond to logic; the profoundly disturbed parent not to be profoundly disturbed and to give unconditional love.

MY ADULTHOOD HAS been about recuperating. There was no compulsion to give life to anyone else because I was depleted. There was nothing to give.

When someone said to me, "You would be a good mother," he or she were speaking about a possibility so distant, it didn't merit reflection. As if he or she had said, "You would be a good teacher." Or "a good person to travel with." I took it as flattery, nothing more.

By forty-five, I had accepted that I would not have children. And this didn't feel like a loss. My mother desperately wanted to have a child. She wanted someone to cleave to her. Having a child was insurance. A lifetime of companionship.

THERE IS A story my mother told me throughout my childhood. Whether I wanted to hear it or not. It was about what had happened to her when she was a little girl, and I listened with attentiveness and curiosity. But it was never edited for the audience of a child. It was brutal, and when I got older I realized she wasn't telling it to me, she was telling it because she had to. It served one purpose. The listener should feel bad for her. It was repeated again and again, and still to this day she tells it because it is the excuse for her behavior and the explanation for why she is who she is. It is the story of her victimhood. The story of her abandonment. The story of her life.

WHEN SHE WAS seven, her mother and father, whose marriage was over, placed her in a boarding school that she hated. Her father—street-smart and a hard worker—had no time for her. Her mother—intellectual, friendly, cultured, a teacher—married another man. In my mother's story, the other man is the villain, lacking any redeeming qualities. He forced my grandmother to choose. He wanted a new family and he didn't want my mother to be a part of it. Her mother married Joe and they moved to a house and lived in the northern Manhattan neighborhood of Inwood, specifically in Park Terrace. Joe and Mae, my grandmother, had three children (my mother's half-siblings) and my mother was thrown away.

And so my mother's mother left her in the Dickensian boarding school and went on to have a loving family that she wasn't a part of. She was discarded, in this sad story, alone at school over holidays when neither her father (who was working) nor her mother (who was busy with her new husband and family) cared to include her.

My mother would point out how fortunate I was to have a mother who wanted me around. "At least I don't throw you away," she'd say. Pain was her province. My grandmother, as my mother repeated frequently, scarred her for life.

IT COULD HAPPEN at any time. I would hear my mother shout, "Do you want me to end up like Aunt Moll?" I knew then that my mother was on the phone with her mother. Aunt Moll was an alcoholic. I never met her. She died before I was born. She was my grandmother's sister and I knew that she had a sad life. That she had fallen or jumped out a window, from an apartment building in New York.

When my mother needed my grandmother to tend to her, she threatened to jump out a window, like Aunt Moll. She could always get to Grandma with that one.

"Is that what you want, Mae? Because that's what will happen."

My mother called her mother by her first name during these outbursts. It was a verbal slap. Spoken with bitterness. "Mae" was the horrible mother who owed her and who would have to pay with infinite time and attention. "Mom" or "Mommy" was the patient obedient mother whose cheerful personality was admired and adored—the mommy she could laugh with until they were both in tears.

IN THE STORY of my mother's life, her salvation was becoming an artist—a poet. She unshackled herself in her poems, met my father, and had a child. The one true miracle of her life.

I was born to erase her past. There was a vacancy that had to be filled. Having a child was driven by a need to quell the emptiness. She couldn't have known this at the time.

"You won't know what it means to love until you have a child," she says.

I am in my forties when she says this. I stay silent. Holidays, her birthday, weekends—denying her time with a grandchild would yield epic conflict. I couldn't see how to avoid it. Other than to cancel it out entirely.

· · ·

WE ARE ON the bottom of the ocean in a canyon of coral. Mario hugs me from above and holds my arms in place in a way to force me to be still. There is a narrow passageway that requires neutral buoyancy. To pass through, we need to have a straight propulsion from his fins. This does not allow me to move or flail about. This hold also keeps the equipment together so nothing will get caught on the coral. At the end of the passage, he discovers the regulator is not in my mouth. The tube had gotten snagged and was yanked out, and when this happened, as we continued through the passageway, I held my breath. It didn't occur to me to put the regulator back in. I couldn't breathe, but I thought I was supposed to hold my breath and that he had knocked the regulator out of my mouth on purpose.

"Why would I do that?" We have come up to the surface and there is a horrified look on his face as he says this, because it would mean he was trying to kill me. But I don't see it that way. I'd thought he was trying to protect me.

He is upset because I could have died. He can't believe that I didn't know I would need air underwater in order to breathe.

MY SURVIVAL INSTINCTS come to the surface in other areas. Spotting the cracks so I know where I can tread. This is my reflex. There is no instruction booklet. Only I know how to fend her off, hold her back, back her down

—and these impulses are automatic. Will it be a good day or a bad day? I am graceful at sidestepping perilous eventualities.

I had no choice but to exist in the sea that she swam in. It was a fragile ecosystem where the temperature changed without warning. My natural shape was dissolved and I became shapeless. A plankton drifting in the current of her expectations. Unable to swim against it. And any attempt to swim away would harm her.

NOW THE GIRLS are beside me. We are floating. The water is still, and one of them begins moving away. She reaches over and places her hand on my upper arm to prevent this from happening. I move her body around so that our heads are touching, and when the other one sees this, she joins in. The three of us rest on the surface of the sea, eyes closed.

15

From 1973 to 1977, I spent every summer living with my father in Bangkok. For two and a half months, I would enter my other life. I slept in my other room with my other stuffed animals and played in the pool with my other set of friends. These friends were the children of expatriates. Kim from Australia, Philip from New Zealand, Justine and Rebecca from America—their father was a journalist for *The Washington Post*. In July we celebrated my half birthday— seven and a half, eight and a half—because my father was unable to be with me for my actual birthday in January. So every year I had two birthdays. My New York birthday and my Bangkok birthday. My Bangkok birthday was the one I looked forward to. As part of the celebration we would go to the Wat Pho temple and see the colossal gold-plated Reclining Buddha. Outside the temple, there were little birds sold individually in tiny wooden cages, and as my father explained the Buddhist idea of making merit, he would take out ten baht and purchase a bird in a cage. Then I would hold it up toward the sky, open the latch, and set it free.

Sometimes we would go to a congested neighborhood for sticky rice and chicken satay. Live chickens would walk along on the semipaved sidewalks. We'd go to the floating market, where rickety canoes piled high with tropical fruits—mangosteens and rambutans, pyramids of bananas and tangerines—drifted along the canal. The boats floated along the khlongs, guided by women in pointed straw hats. We took weekend trips to the south. Pattaya was an untouched beach with only a handful of hotels, and Chiang Mai, up north, was where elephants and giant hippos outnumbered people. My father had a sky-blue Chrysler Valiant and a driver. The driver taught me to say "stop here" in Thai. It sounded like *jaw teeny*, and I would blurt this out while he was driving until my father told me not to do that because it confused the driver. I'd do it anyway and it made me giggle.

In Bangkok we would take samlors, the three-wheeled taxis resembling a rickshaw, but with a motor. The samlors were colored bright pink, like cotton candy. Back then they ran on diesel fuel and sounded like lawn mowers. As we waited for the light to change, the backseat, covered in plastic, would rumble and heat up. The blazing heat and sultry air would cause the back of my thighs to sweat so that when I stood up at the end of the ride, I would have to peel myself off the seat.

I had unofficially adopted an elephant, Bimbo, who lived at the Dusit Thani hotel. On weekends my father and I would get to ride him around the pool. In photos of this period, he is holding me tight and I am safe in his arms, smiling.

MY FATHER WAS good at good-byes. Emotion was real and undiluted. At the end of the summer we would stand inside the departures terminal at the international airport in Bangkok, and he would take me as far as he could go. I would make the prolonged voyage back to New York with a different companion after Kiki died. The airlines would not permit a child to travel such a long distance alone. One year it was my grandmother, my father's mother, who had spent the summer with me. Another year, it was a colleague from my father's law firm who had to make a trip to America. I wore a laminated card that year around my neck with my name and age, in case we were separated in Copenhagen during the layover. By the age of nine, I'd been around the world five times.

AT THE AIRPORT, my father would kneel down on the concrete floor in front of me so that we were at eye level. His navy-blue Izod Lacoste shirt was drenched with sweat, and there were dark pools of perspiration under his arms and in a circle on his back. He had tears in his eyes; I felt nervous that if he blinked, they would roll out, and I didn't want that because I didn't want to see him cry. He pulled me in close for a hug and would say something funny that made me laugh. He was never afraid to cry in front of me. And he would choke back tears through a series of finals. Final call for the flight, final check of the ticket. "Okay, kiddo," he says sweetly, "that's you." And as he says this, his voice breaks. He gives me a final hug. There were promises. To see me again soon. To write every single day. And he did.

. . .

THERE WAS A mossy green wooden cabinet in my bedroom in New York. The top part of the cabinet had shelves for clothes. The bottom half had two doors that stayed shut only when the key was turned in the keyhole. It was stuffed with red and pale blue airmail envelopes. Hundreds of them. I loved the bright-colored stamps that decorated the front. Some of them had elephants and golden palaces. These were the letters Josie read out loud to me before I went to sleep. They were my bedtime story. They would begin "Hi, Pal," or "Hi, Kiddo," and they would always include how much my father missed me. How he was thinking of me. Every minute of every day. He would ask questions about my schoolwork and friends at school— refer to them by name. He would use only vocabulary words that I could understand. Mentioning things we had to look forward to when we saw each other. And every letter would end with a special sign-off. I love you more than all the grains of sand on the beach. I love you more than all the stars in the sky. I love you more than all the fish in the sea.

AT THE AIRPORT in Bangkok, my father was never al-lowed to walk me to the gate because to get past secu-rity he needed a boarding pass. So we'd have to say our good-byes in a terminal full of moving strangers. It was the mid-seventies and the airport had no air-conditioning. The heat was dense, and my father, tan and athletic, was always damp from the sweat. I flinched when he stood up and leaned down to give me a final kiss on the top of my head. "Daddy," I said, "don't drip on me."

AFTER SPENDING TIME with my father in Bangkok, I never wanted to return to New York. But any attempt to extend my visit caused my mother to panic. She would insist she couldn't live without me. "I'm having a nervous breakdown. I haven't seen my child in months. I can't go another day without her."

At the end of August when I was seven years old, my mother and Josie met me at JFK airport and we rode back to 180 in the taxi. As soon as we reached the building, my mother dropped me off and said she was continuing on. I told her I wanted her to come upstairs so we could call my father and tell him that I had arrived safely. She agreed to this but went out as soon as we were done. I fell asleep, and when I woke up the next morning, I called Rita.

Rita answered the phone and I told her my mother wasn't with me. "I could have stayed with Daddy for three more weeks, but Mommy wanted me home and now she isn't even here. She went out to dinner and she never came back."

FOR THREE MONTHS when I was nine, my father, between jobs, rented a furnished apartment at the Surrey, a hotel in New York. We strolled along Madison Avenue holding hands. I could talk to him every day after school if I wanted. On weekends he took me to the movies; we went jogging in Central Park and ate hot dogs at Nathan's. I never wanted that time to end.

But my mother reminded me it wasn't permanent. "What kind of father leaves his child to move to the other side of the world? If he loved you, he'd live in New York."

"He didn't leave me." I'd run to my room and slam the door.

I had a constant companion who would console me. Smashy. Smashy looked like an oven mitt covered with cherry-red synthetic fur. He wasn't a stuffed animal because he wasn't an animal and he wasn't stuffed. He was a hand puppet. Similar to a Muppet. An ancestor to Elmo, with no lower body. My father had given me Smashy as a half-birthday present when I'd last been in Bangkok and turned eight and a half. And from the moment he arrived in my life, he was my best friend. My father accepted this as fact. When we went out to dinner, Smashy had his own chair at the table. My father placed a menu in front of him, addressed him directly, and asked what he felt like eating. When we talked on the phone, my father suggested I put Smashy on the line so that he could ask questions about what I was reading and what my favorite subject in school was and which classmates I liked and which I didn't.

During the time my father was in New York, I was occasionally allowed to have sleepovers with him on weekends. I had my own room there, and even though it was a hotel, I pretended it was our apartment. I pretended he had custody of me and that I didn't have to leave him to return to my mother. At night he tucked me into bed, and lying next to me, with his head on the pillow, was Smashy. My father tucked him in as well. I asked for a glass of water with a straw, and when I was done my father held the straw in Smashy's mouth so that he could have a sip, too. The three of us talked about visiting the monkey forests or spinning around in the giant teacups at Coney Island, and when he left the room and turned out the light, I told Smashy I wished that when we woke up in the morning, we'd discover my father had found a job in New York. And that he'd moved into an apartment and was never going to have to leave.

ONE AFTERNOON IT was raining and the three of us were in a cab on our way back to the hotel. It was a Checker cab and I had placed Smashy on the bumper seat; he was seat-belted in. We got out and my father walked around to the front so that he could pay the driver through the window. I waited on the curb. But just as the cab pulled away, I realized that Smashy had been left behind. My father and I stood for a few seconds, paralyzed, as the unthinkable set in. We raced upstairs and went right to the bedroom, and he began making phone calls. I didn't even unbutton my coat. I just sat next to him while he dialed, holding my breath and whispering, "Please don't let Smashy be gone."

My father stayed on the phone for a very long time.

He spoke quietly, his voice grave and direct: "He's red and fuzzy," but I corrected him, saying "furry," so he repeated: "He's red and furry with a straw sombrero sewn on top of his head."

After a few hours of this, he assured me he wasn't giving up. He put his hands on my shoulders and looked in my eyes. "Don't worry, kiddo, we'll find him." But when I asked, "You promise?" he nodded his head and replied, "I sure hope so."

He told me he was going to go to the cab company and to sit tight—he'd be back soon. I waited. And when my father returned, he walked through the door and I saw that his eyes were tender and that he'd been crying. He took off his blazer and loosened his tie. He came over to me, gave me a hug, sat me down on the couch, and took my hand. When he spoke, his voice cracked. He said he'd tried everything he could. He had looked everywhere. But Smashy was gone. So we sat for a while, just the two of us. I cried more than I'd cried in a very long time, and he cried with me.

A few weeks later, after my father had moved back to Bangkok, Josie told me a special delivery package had arrived. I took it into my room and sat on the floor and opened it up. Wrapped in newspaper was an identical puppet, except that this one had electric-blue fur. There was a note attached in my father's slanted handwriting: "Greetings. Can I live with you? I'm Trashy. Smashy's cousin."

16

People say all the time, "Your father is the nicest man." Local Balinese people will tell me this. How thoughtful he is. How considerate. He can talk to anyone.

"What I loved about your father," Rita told me once, reflecting on her time with him, years later while I was visiting her at her house in Connecticut, "is that he was the most intelligent man I ever met, but he never once made me feel stupid." That his sprawling intellect never bred a sense of superiority is something I admired as well.

I HAVE NEVER heard my father argue with anyone. I have rarely heard him raise his voice. If there is someone he dislikes, he'll say, they are "not my favorite person"—that's as disparaging as it gets.

He didn't argue with my mother. He listened. And when he couldn't listen anymore, he would go out, against her protestations, walk around the block on East 79th Street, and return to 180. We are having breakfast at his house, and as he tells me this, I am surprised that she let him leave. He laughs and says, "Not exactly."

He has blocked out the helplessness he must have felt. Likable people don't warehouse acrimony and bitterness.

·   ·   ·

HE RECALLS THAT for the six years they were married and living in New York, he cannot remember a single evening he spent by himself or with friends. As he says this, I take umbrage at the insouciance of his reflection. I have noticed this with others—as time passes, the memory of my mother's behavior becomes less grainy, the surface is smoothed out, and a fondness for her eccentricity replaces animosity at the struggle to be free of the harassment.

"I remember going to Dallas once for work," my father says. "Maybe two years into the relationship. We'd never been apart for one day. And it felt, I don't know . . ." He smiles, remembering the liberation. "Good. That was the first time I had been away from her."

Every evening they had to be together. There was a party. A dinner. An event. There wasn't an evening together at home, just the two of them. "There was always somebody there," he says. And as he describes the life he had with my mother, it's as though he is telling a story of someone else. Someone who no longer exists. He says there was an argument because he went to Hong Kong on a business trip for two weeks, and when he returned, he'd had enough. "How could you do this to me?" she cried. He moved out and spent the next forty years by himself.

EMILY, MY THERAPIST, once asked me to recall positive memories from childhood. I could talk about time spent with my father in Bangkok that was not turbulent, and when I see photographs of myself with him, I am grinning; in his presence, I was at ease and content. But often these memories were like reciting a poem by heart. I knew the words, but the recitation was devoid of sentiment.

MY FATHER WOULD go jogging every day. He'd been doing this since the early sixties, before it became popular. It seemed messy, an unpleasant sweaty habit, but he jogged every morning. He would jog through the streets of Bangkok, on the beaches of Indonesia, in New York City—he would run around the reservoir in Central Park. When it was winter, he would jog in a T-shirt and shorts. When I asked him why he did this, he said, "Because I am putting miles in the bank." When he was sixty-five, he ran his first New York City Marathon. At eighty-five, he can no longer run, and it's one of the great losses in his life. But he is fit, and the years of exercise bequeathed him good health.

When I think back now to our time together, it was episodic and I knew it would end, but the attention he paid and the love that he gave was solid and true and it left a footprint on my psyche. The happiness miles were logged in the bank.

17

When Rita first told me about the letters she wrote, I wasn't prepared. Neither of us can recall what prompted her to tell me about them or offer them to me to read. I was in my early thirties and living in New York. They arrived in a FedEx envelope with a note:

> *Dearest Ariel,*
>
> *As you read through these, it may seem like you're watching a television soap opera in which you are the star. I sincerely hope this experience doesn't upset you. You may get some laughs from what you read. You will surely be angry and cry either from a recalled joy or a remembered sadness. Sending these letters is a bit of a risk. I've no idea how the adult Ariel will feel reading intimate things of her life as a child.*
>
> *Love, Rita*

HER LETTERS TO my father were typed single space on a manual typewriter. There is barely any room on the page not covered in print. There are hefty paragraphs and few indentations. Most of the letters are more than one page. Two or three pages each. The volume of correspondence is staggering. There are weeks at a time when she wrote every day. December 18 is four pages. December 19 is two. Then there will be a break and the narrative will pick up again one week later.

THE LETTERS BEGIN in 1973 and end in 1976. She had used carbon sets so that there were copies. A one-time-use carbon sheet was attached to a tissue-thin piece of paper. She slipped it behind the regular bond paper and an automatic copy was made.

The paper from the carbon set is lightweight and durable. It is used for permanent records. It is impervious to age and elements that would destroy it; resistant to oil and grease. What happened could not be deleted. Could not be smeared. The transparency was undeniable.

When I opened the FedEx envelope and held the letters in my hand, I was holding a black-and-white archive. She had traced my childhood onto the page.

I TOOK THE letters into my bathroom in New York and sat on the cold tile floor, with my back resting against the ceramic bathtub. I closed the door, even though I lived alone and no one would interrupt. The pile was about an inch and a half thick. I began to read but then had to stop. It took me months to get through them all. I got no laughs from what I read. I did not cry from a recalled joy or a remembered sadness, as Rita had noted.

I read them as though reviewing documents that would serve as evidence in a trial. I read about a little girl who had to navigate an unsafe world, a world without boundaries. This child was left alone most of the time—if not physically, emotionally. And then every once in a while, it would hit me that that child was me.

WHAT I SAW was a diplomat. At seven years old I was strategizing. Understanding that asserting myself was not just useless but harmful. It didn't matter if I was right or wrong, what mattered is that I didn't make it worse. What mattered was making sure my mother was taken care of.

The letters are my ally. Above all else, they confirmed what I knew: my anger was justified. The distrust that had shaped who I became had a substantiated origin.

MY MOTHER MADE me doubt and question my perceptions. The loving and warm persona that followed the tirades confused and destabilized me. I wanted a witness. An ally. To verify. To have proof.

Someone I could turn to and say, "This happened, didn't it?"

Someone who could see the transformation I saw.

"I have a right to be angry, don't I? I don't trust her," I say.

Only I didn't say this. Because I was seven years old and I didn't know yet that's how I felt. And not trusting one's mother is, on a cellular level, unjust.

I needed to be heard and kept hoping she would hear me. As a child, it was too overwhelming to believe that she couldn't recognize reality. My craving for her to be different was powerful. It inoculated me against the tumult.

I descended deep within myself, far away to a place in the future. Where things would make sense and right was right and wrong was wrong. I was able to crawl away from my rage.

But I never crawled away far enough.

MY FATHER DIDN'T respond to what Rita wrote, though he acknowledged the letters when he received them. Why did she write? She loved me, she loved him, and she believed he needed to know. He expressed his gratitude that she was informing him. I imagine him reading the letters while in Thailand, half a world away from 180 East 79th Street. What could he do? The circumstances were beyond his control.

While she was sending him these meticulous dispatches,

he was writing to me directly. Beautiful letters were his way of giving loving and caring thoughts to counter the angst. Rita writing to my father, my father writing to me, my mother writing poetry. Everyone was writing their way out of the helplessness.

"How could we all be true to ourselves and still get out of the quagmire?" Rita asks. We are older; forty years have passed. We are standing in Grand Central Station before she catches the train home to Connecticut. "I was never able to answer that. Perhaps your father couldn't either. And you, dear child, were in the middle."

THE LETTERS ARE now in a maroon folder. I have brought them with me to Bali. I am seated at a table outside when the folder is suddenly blown open by a gust of wind. Pages are hoisted up into the air, swirling in all directions. I reach for a nearby book and slam it on top of the folder so that the remaining letters are secure. I bolt from the chair to pursue the others. Eight or nine of them have scattered and dance in the air, circling me in a whirlpool of words. I pounce, leaping after my past, clutching at it, securing it down, refusing to let it blow away.

18

The year is 1976. My mother has appeared in an article in *People* magazine. She talks about her glamorous life as a poet. She says that unlike Sylvia Plath and Anne Sexton, she stays sane by connecting with other women's concerns. "Depression is an indulgence," she cheerfully tells the reporter. In her bathroom, the mirrored medicine cabinet above the porcelain sink is stocked with a variety of sepia-colored prescription pill bottles. Tranquilizers prescribed by her psychiatrist after or before one of her "nervous breakdowns." There are a dozen of these bottles. Medications she takes for a while, then stops. The prescriptions were useless, she said, causing her to act crazy. "I'm not taking anything ever again," she tells me. "Except the occasional Valium."

In the magazine, there is a striking photograph of her sitting on the piano bench leaning against the Steinway grand. She is dressed in a sleeveless black evening gown with a slit that goes up to just below her hip bone. Silver stiletto sandals on her feet. Her hair has been styled by a hairdresser and looks shiny and sleek. The caption says she has been called "a blond Sophia Loren" by some admirers. Behind the piano there is a door that is closed. It is my bedroom.

The other photo is of her skipping rope in Central Park

without a bra. Off to the left, I can be seen seated on the ground, watching her play. I am in the article, too. My room is described in detail as my mother comments on how it's filled with books and poems she wrote for me—one to make table manners and chores more palatable. "She's my daughter and my best friend," she says. She has said this all my life.

"I SHARE WITH you, you share with me. That's what mothers and daughters do." It's a command, not a choice. Withholding is a rejection. "I'm your best friend," she announces.

But I don't know that. All I know is that I have never responded that she is my best friend, too. What's not written in the article is that I have never spent a single day alone with my mother. Ever.

THE THIRD PHOTO is of my mother wearing a silver fox fur Dr. Zhivago pillbox hat and reading from a book of her poems. She holds one arm out in the air in an animated pose. She would wear that hat when her hair was dirty, often putting it on when she woke up and leaving it on all day. When she took off the hat, I was embarrassed by her matted, messy hair. In the photo she is surrounded by a dozen friends—some seated on my bed, others standing or leaning against the windowsill. There is a cardboard cutout of her latest novel. In the foreground, there is a baby's pram used for dolls. The photo was taken in my bedroom, where often her guests would congregate during her parties, invading my space whether I wanted them to or not. My mother would enter to give an impromptu reading of her poetry. My bedroom was a sanctuary for everyone but me.

19

When I first met Donald, my mother's boyfriend, I was six years old. He was drinking then. Dewar's on the rocks. I see him sitting with a drink in his hand on the white slipcovered sofa in the living room at 180. His gold pinkie ring gently tapping the side of the glass. He is waiting, patiently, for my mother to get dressed.

I didn't like him at first. He was another one of my mother's boyfriends who occupied her attention. I needed her and she needed him. But in time, I became as attached to him as she was. He stopped drinking when I was ten, and after that, I could rely on him. He tried his best to come to my mother's rescue, but it was impossible not to disappoint her. With me, it was different. Donald never let me down.

DONALD WAS IN his late sixties when they got together. She playfully joked about how he was a lothario, a ladies' man, a playboy, and it wasn't entirely untrue. Women adored Donald because in New York City he stood out. He looked like Charles Bronson, with the rugged reserve of a seasoned cowboy. He was a savvy, successful entrepreneur who'd made a fortune as the founder of Tad's

Steaks, a chain of restaurants he started in 1957. This endeavor earned him the title "grandfather of the fast-food business." My mother saw his ingenuity as a talent; he created something from nothing. The way she turned a blank page into a poem, he turned a steak into an empire.

DONALD CAME FROM a different world, one in which common sense prevailed. He was what my mother called a straight shooter. No nonsense. He didn't maneuver. He wasn't neurotic. He was a shrewd businessman with a level-headedness that extended to how he operated in life. My mother says, "I listen to everything Donald tells me. He's the smartest man I know."

He grew up in North Dakota, the son of a cattle rancher, and his work ethic and self-made success defined him. He often spoke about how no one ever gave him anything in life and he tried to rein in my mother's belief that the world owed her. He was, above all else, tolerant. When it came to her, this was his weakness.

DONALD MOVED THROUGH my mother's world with consummate ease. He was pleasant and gracious and his sense of humor was raunchy and often lewd—he loved dirty jokes.

His appearance was, like his manner, dependable. He would wear denim jackets and shirts with a Western bolo tie—braided leather with a metal tip. Unless he was in a suit, I don't remember ever seeing him in anything other than blue jeans.

DONALD FOSTERED A feeling in my mother of being taken care of. He was her benefactor, boyfriend, accountant, therapist, adviser, father, confidant, champion, and friend. He found her amusing, endearing, outrageous, and "one of a kind."

MY MOTHER IS in the bedroom getting dressed to go out for the evening, which means most likely she is running a bath while sitting naked on her bed, talking on the phone. Donald doesn't yell at her to hurry up. He doesn't stand up, walk to the bedroom to check on her progress. He just sits and waits until she appears. The most he will do is call out, "The reservation was for eight o'clock."

At eight-thirty, she will appear. She looks glamorous when she is dressed up. Her hair is blown dry and she is wearing high heels from Charles Jourdan and a lavender silk dress. She smells of Joy perfume. He will take her out to dinner, probably to Nicola's, Parma, or Elaine's.

Sometimes, before they went out, my mother would come in my bedroom to say goodnight. She looked beautiful. I would say, "Hold footie," and she would sit on the edge of my bed and hold my bare foot for a few minutes before she left. In those minutes she was there for me in the way that I needed. I felt reassured by her.

LATER THAT EVENING, when they return to the apartment, the argument begins. Donald tells her he doesn't want to sleep over. This was something he'd let her know ahead of time, but that she'd ignored. She talks him into coming upstairs to discuss it further. And at the point he decides he's had enough, he gets up to go home.

From my bedroom I overhear the raised voices.

"I'm leaving," he states.

"No, you're not!"

She rushes him like a wildebeest, to block this from happening. He shoves her aside, but it doesn't deter her. They are both drunk, unaware of the volume or velocity of their savage aggression.

Donald is unable to defuse the explosion. He is willful.

"Move out of the way, woman," he commands. Sharply. Dismissive. This makes it worse.

The shoving sounds frighten me the most. The scuffing of the shoes on the hardwood floors. The tussling noises are a violent explosive dance.

"No!" I hear the stomp of her foot. "You promised!"

He didn't promise.

"I'm leaving," he says. "Too bad."

. . .

THIS WAS HOW the bedlam began. Sometimes before a party started, earlier in the afternoon, I would check with my mother to see if Donald was sleeping over that night. Because the nights he agreed to sleep over were negotiated ahead of time, and when I knew in advance it was a sleepover night, I felt less anxious. I could relax. But often, as the night went on, she would provoke an argument and it would escalate and the verbal attack would become intolerable and then he would change his mind. That's when the assault would start.

Nothing will contain it. Their breathing is too loud and the recklessness is too frenzied. They are determined. Uninhibited and out of control.

I squeeze the pillow over my head and shut my eyes so tight that they ache. I can still hear the shoving, the sliding and slipping around, as they wrestle and he struggles to regain his balance and composure and pry himself away from her clutches.

"*Owwwww,* you're pulling my hair out!" she wails. "You're killing me—you're killing me!" There is more shoving. "I'm bleeding—*owwwwww*—ARIEL, CALL THE POLICE!"

I jump up out of my bed and fling open my door. I see his hair in her hand—clumps of his white hair would be on the floor. His face is scratched, blood drawn by her long red fingernails. I stand frozen in my nightgown.

"Please, Mommy, let him go—let him go home!" I plead. "Let him go home!"

I am afraid for his safety, not hers.

She barricades the front door, not allowing him to leave. Her bathrobe is open and untied and Donald is fully dressed with his jacket on. He is trying to move her out of the way to no avail.

"You're not leaving me!"

My mother is unaware of my presence as I stand by, watching her try to push him back to her bedroom. It is a lurch of graceless abandon.

"Mommy, stop!" I shout.

"Let go of me!" She spits this at Donald, who is trying to protect himself.

"Stop!" I shout.

I am a phantom presence. Standing there sobbing, as though I'm not making a sound.

The fighting is feral. She bites his hand as he tries to silence her. He tries to peel her off him.

"Call the police!" she screams again. "He's trying to kill me!"

"Stop!" I shout, hysterical. "Please stop!"

MY MOTHER HUGS his calves so that he can't move, but he drags her across the carpet to the elevator. The gates open and Charlie, the elevator man who works the night shift, waits as my mother and Donald continue to brawl.

"I'm going with you!" my mother shouts, pursuing him. Once the elevator doors shut, I am unable to calm down. Josie appears in her nightgown and takes me to her room off the kitchen; I crawl into bed with her so that I can sleep. I take slow, deep breaths to stop my heart from beating too fast, and she pats the back of my head in steady strokes. I am shaking and Josie's presence—her body next to mine—helps to settle me down. I lie next to her, relieved that my mother is out of the apartment, that the raging scene is over. I close my eyes, hoping she stays away and spends the night at Donald's.

THE FIGHT WITH Donald would continue in the lobby and then out on the sidewalk in front of the building. In the morning, when I went to my mother's room to wake her up, I would know, if she wasn't there, that she had insisted on staying the night at Donald's house, and unable to get rid of her and weary from the effort, he had relented.

I WOULD LEAVE for school, and when I returned in the afternoon, she would be in her bedroom, happily typing away. She would wave me over, greet me with an effusive smile, and demand an affectionate greeting. "Ariel, darling, love of my life, come give Mommy a kiss! I am so happy to see you. How was school today?"

"It was fine," I'd reply in a brooding voice, conveying an indifference a nine-year-old doesn't yet understand.

She didn't appreciate my attitude. "Don't you want to give Mommy a kiss hello?"

I'd shake my head.

"She never kisses me," she'd complain to whoever was around. "I can't understand it."

20

How could someone with so much feel so deprived? You look around at all the things you were given. Things that were purchased. Chairs that were reupholstered. You are told that the attention was there. That care was given, deeply felt. Renouncing this must be a failure of character. My force of rebellion is unwarranted. But emotional truth is at odds with reality. There were privileges, yes. Education, inspiration, encouragement, support. And there were riches. But the riches didn't compensate. The privilege didn't mollify. They were there, but they were decorative. The turmoil couldn't be refunded. The memories couldn't be reupholstered. Privilege was never about neighborhood. It was never about status. Or items. Or things.

PRIVILEGE WOULD HAVE been falling asleep at night without fear about what would happen as the night went on. Privilege would have been not being woken up with terror. Privilege would have been not having to disown negative feelings or suppress them because those feelings were not permitted. Not being punished for responding appropriately to inappropriate behavior. Privilege would have been not being held responsible for the stability of my mother's psyche. Privilege would have been stability. An indemnity from being idealized one minute, devalued the next. Privilege would have been a parent capable of empathy. A protector.

SHE EMPHASIZES THE world she has provided for me and my lack of gratitude. It disturbs her. She tells me, "Count your blessings. You don't know how good you have it." She says this as a reproach. I have taken advantage of her. I am a taker. "You don't appreciate what you have. Do I not give you everything you've ever wanted?"

There is the list. Everything is on it from the day I was born. A penthouse apartment. A bedroom of my own, with books and toys and a closet full of shoes. A private school. Piano lessons. A beautiful childhood. Happy. Not like hers. I had an exceptional mother. Who wanted me. An artist. A poet. A mentor. A friend. I was surrounded by artistic freedom and an affluence of advantage and opportunity. I was not living in squalor. I was not naked. I was not hungry.

The catalog of what she has given includes time, attention, and love. And what she has paid for. The numbers seem inflated, but I can't argue. It was her money. She did spend it. I took from her. The appreciation has to be infinite. Any complaint is baseless. "Stop whining," she says. "Don't be a victim."

·   ·   ·

SHE SACRIFICED HER career for me. She sacrificed her personal life for me. She could have had, she could have done, she could have saved, she could have gone. This is her narrative. It is indisputable. She gave up everything. *Everything.* For me.

HER DISTORTIONS ARE not always detectable to others. Disputing them requires a special magnifying glass. An X-ray of the truth. I am reluctant to explain myself for fear of whining. The adversity, when measured, feels slight.

IN 2011, I was commissioned to do an interview with a woman who had survived the Holocaust, seeking refuge from the Nazis in the sewers of Lvov, Poland. The memoir she'd written had been made into a film nominated that year for Best Foreign Film at the Academy Awards. During the war, she had been forced with her family to go underground to hide, and with the help of a Catholic man who worked in the sewer, they were able to live for fourteen months in the city sewer's system. She was seven years old at the time.

I took a train to her home on the North Shore of Long Island, a two-hour ride from Manhattan. What was it that compelled her to overcome her tragic circumstances? The message of her memoir was life-affirming. She did not view herself as a victim. She did not feel handicapped by her past. I need to know: what was it that made this possible?

It was a frigid winter day and I could see my breath when I stepped off the train onto the outdoor platform of the station. The overcast sky put me at ease. I began the walk from the train station to her house. She had suggested I take a taxi, but I wanted to stroll through a suburban neighborhood and embrace the anonymity of passing by the conventional landscape where no one knew where I was. I walked briskly, avoiding the ice on the ground. A series of roads and hills and nondescript modest houses.

We spoke for a while. The tragedy of her childhood did not diminish her. It did not break her. It was a painful period of her life, but the legacy was not painful. She told me her story, and afterward, as I ride the train back to Manhattan, I fixate on what shaped her sensibility.

Throughout the fourteen months the family spent underground, her mother and father were always optimistic. Despite the uncertainty, the inhuman conditions, the lack of fresh air, the stench, and the threat of death, they never gave in to despair. She felt endangered by circumstances, but protected by love. This, I believed, was the formula for not being crippled by anger. A consistent optimism that was indestructible. It enabled her to defy the circumstances.

· · ·

I HAD FRIENDS whose families owned cosmic Park Avenue apartments and country houses in the Hamptons. When I visited them, what I envied was not their properties, but a chance to spend time in a home without conflict. I had friends whose families lived in walk-ups on narrow streets in darkened neighborhoods and whose bedroom windows faced brick walls. When I visited them, what I envied was a chance to spend time in a home without feeling on edge. Serenity was affluence. Consistency was opulence. I didn't care about the neighborhood. The status. Or the paintings on the wall. I valued moments that were not fraught and tumultuous. Time with my father. Time with Rita. Privilege was when I was not saturated with despair that didn't belong to me. When I could be my own person and enjoy the advantage that others came by naturally: feeling safe in my home.

21

In the New York of the 1960s, my mother moved in a circle of acclaimed artistic achievers. Poets and painters and authors and artists who to varying degrees were out for themselves. Their absence of humility was an asset. The advertising of oneself wasn't considered crude, but venerated. In that febrile scene, works of art excused misconduct. Narcissism flourished. Bad behavior was indulged. Poets were dramatic and vivacious and histrionic. Being an exhibitionist was encouraged. It was an exciting time. That's what I was told.

But for me, those days were a disruption. I didn't see exceptional artists, I saw grown-ups who behaved childishly. Boisterous, inconsiderate people who never left the party. I would come out of my bedroom, exasperated. "When is everyone leaving?" Indifferent faces would stare back at me. Who is this demanding seven-year-old interrupting our good time? My mother apologized for my churlish behavior. "I'm sorry my daughter is so rude."

These people weren't my allies. And their accomplishments did not exonerate them. They were my mother's guests who made too much noise on a school night.

·   ·   ·

WHERE MY MOTHER fit in the pantheon is hard to determine. She wasn't at the epicenter, but she wasn't on the margins either. She was highly regarded and befriended the literary heavyweights. There were the artifacts. The signed Lichtenstein that was presented as a wedding gift. The watercolor by Henry Miller for when I was born. Robert Lowell's notes on her poems. Philip Roth and Saul Bellow were guests at the house and praised her work.

These associations were validations. I was too young to know why this acceptance mattered or to care. And then when I was old enough to care, I didn't.

"I want a mommy-mommy." I would say. "Someone who cuts the crusts of my bread." She would laugh at the banality of this. And remind me how fortunate I was to have her, an artist, as my mother.

WHEN NORMAN MAILER ran for mayor of New York in 1969, my mother hosted a fund-raiser for him at the apartment. I was a baby and my father, recalling this evening, said, "It probably raised fifty dollars. But that wasn't the point."

Growing up, my mother frequently encouraged me to tell people Norman Mailer was my "godfather." I was reluctant to reveal this because it didn't feel real. I had met Mailer once or twice, and he was cordial to me. We didn't have an intimate connection, and telling people that he was my godfather felt unnatural and weird. Later, when I was working at the *Sunday Times*, Mailer had written a piece for the magazine, and when my editor mentioned to him that I worked there and asked about his being my godfather, he confessed that he had been "dragooned" into it. When my editor told me this, I felt I had been implicated in a version of my life that didn't belong to me.

ONLY IT DID. Because my mother would use her connections to help me, whether I wanted this help or not. She persuaded Mailer to write a college recommendation letter. I have no memory of the letter, no copy of it, and how much influence it wielded is unknown. "If it weren't for me asking Norman Mailer to write your recommendation letter, you would never had gotten into college," she said. I owed her. Although if I had said, "I want to go to college in Spain and be on my own," I knew she would not have solicited a recommendation for that.

I OFTEN WENT to Elaine's with my mother and witnessed her in action. One night she approached a table in the front of the restaurant where a Famous Writer with White Hair (was it Joseph Heller?) was sitting and interrupted his dinner with friends. He did not invite her to sit down, but she took a seat anyway. I continued on to a table in the back with Donald and waited for her to join us. Elaine had to usher

her away. There was an uncomfortable feeling of knowing my mother had no idea she was being a nuisance.

ANDY WARHOL SHOWED up at the wedding reception when she and my father got married on New Year's Day, 1966. Several members of the Velvet Underground were there as well. She drew people in with her mesmeric appeal, then drove them away with magnificent need.

For me, the message was clear. Instability was a natural state of being. An artist was allowed to bend the rules. It was a mandate. And she was surrounded by others who, like her, nested in the turbulence of living.

Masters of emotional jujitsu.

I WOULD SEE some of these people in the living room at 180 at my mother's parties. I didn't know who they were. Warhol was a spooky figure with white hair and a black turtleneck who didn't smile.

"Ariel, come out and say hello to Andy," my mother said, opening the door to my bedroom. He looked stricken.

WHEN I GOT older, my mother would get upset that I didn't promote myself enough.

"You're shooting yourself in the foot," she would say in response to my refusal to follow her directions. "You're making a huge mistake."

"Okay, I'm making a mistake."

"Why don't you listen to me?" This would be followed with a list of people to contact. "Call him and tell him you're my daughter."

I knew it was coming from a well-meaning desire to see me succeed. She was trying to help.

"I'm not comfortable doing that."

"You have to sell yourself. Haven't you learned anything? That's the way it works. How did you get so *genteel*?"

She was a dedicated and electric self-promoter and didn't see it as an unattractive quality. Unless it appeared in others. "She's nothing but a self-promoter," she'd say with disgust.

The fraught destiny for poets was one she alternately accepted and rejected depending on the day. The fragility and torture were worth the anguish. It was a gift. The fragility and torture were something she wouldn't wish on her worst enemy. It was a curse.

ON WEEKNIGHTS I lie in bed, alone in my room, listening to my mother's dinner parties and hoping the guests will leave at midnight. As she has promised. I have school the next day, and this was the agreement. She would have buffets. Sometimes she would have sit-down dinners that turned into buffets because she'd lose track of how many people she had invited and guests would end up eating paella out of silver-plated ashtrays using wooden salad spoons. One time she handed someone a trowel in place of a fork. He didn't seem that alarmed. He remarked that he had never used a gardening tool as a dining utensil, but she told him there was a first time for everything and not to be so middle class.

IF THERE WEREN'T enough seats at the table, she'd improvise. The piano bench, the step stool—sometimes she'd turn a garbage pail upside down or send someone into my bedroom to borrow my desk chair. "There's plenty of room over there!" she'd shout and point to the windowsill. Twenty people around a table for twelve. Scrambled eggs when she ran out of veal. Even when she'd emerge from her bedroom wrapped in a towel and covered in bubbles, nearly two hours after her guests had arrived, her apology would be so whimsical and flamboyant it would overshadow her lateness. People were entertained.

FROM THE OTHER side of the door, I hear the unruly guests laughing. My mother's laughter was always the loudest. She was a sublime storyteller. Weaving her crafty antics into a self-deprecating tale that lampooned her inappropriate behavior.

I get up and open my door, which is right off the living

room. I stand in my nightgown and angrily announce, "It's midnight. Can everyone go home now?" They ignore me and she clinks her wineglass with a knife, "Everyone! Everyone! We have to be quiet! Ariel has to get up for school tomorrow."

She reassures me. "Fifteen more minutes. Then everyone will go home."

"You promised everyone would go home at midnight."

"They're leaving soon."

No one leaves. I shut the door and return to my bed, place the pillow over my head, and hope that it stays quiet. For a while it does, and in this pause, I try to make myself fall asleep. Then a piercing shriek of "Ahhhh" from my mother's uninhibited enjoyment breaks the silence. I get up again, and open my door.

"You said fifteen minutes!" I shout. There are half a dozen lingering guests, lounging on the sofa and sitting on the floor. Those who have no motivation to depart.

"You're too loud. I can't sleep."

"Shhhhhh," my mother coaxes her guests. Time passes. I repeat. And repeat. And repeat.

SYLVIA MILES HAS come into my bedroom unannounced to smoke and complain. "Your mother isn't even dressed yet," she says in a brassy nasal voice. I am eight years old. She has an elaborate hat on her head with a shiny brooch pinned to the side and a black fishnet veil that goes to the bridge of her nose. Her lipstick is shrill and red, and there is a smudge of it on her shiny white teeth. She clutches at her feathered boa over her leopard-print blouse.

"She told me to be here at eight sharp, and she's still not even ready! I need to use the john."

I am doing my homework. It's a school night and my mother's party is under way. It's a special occasion, another one, and the rule of No Parties on Weeknights has been amended. The music is playing—Fred Astaire singing "Puttin' On the Ritz"—and there is a scratch on the record. A line in the song repeats on a loop until someone walks over to the turntable, lifts up the needle, and moves it along.

SYLVIA DIDN'T LIKE children and made that clear. She would tell me that, and I'm not sure if she noticed I was a child. "Ariel," she whined, "can you please go check on your mother and tell her I'm waiting?"

"I'm doing my homework."

"Who *are* these people?" She was wasting her time.

My mother's friendship with Sylvia seemed built on an intense dislike for each other. They'd been friends a long time. They had too much in common.

"SYLVIA!" I'D HEAR my mother shout into the phone. "Just make an appearance. It's my birthday and I want you

to be there. It's not going to kill you." She would entice
Sylvia with the promise of someone important who would
be at the party, knowing this would make her think that if
she didn't show up, she might be missing out. Once Sylvia
got to the party, she would express her dissatisfaction with
the crowd. The famous director my mother had promised
would be there had come and gone.

"Who is this 'Sandman' person?" she'd ask me.

My mother had lifted up the rug in the living room and
Howard "Sandman" Sims was sprinkling Uncle Ben's rice
on the hardwood floor. He was an old black tap dancer from
vaudeville, and my mother was writing a play based on his life.

What I knew about Sandman Sims is that the rice he
spread on the floor amplified the sound of his sliding
across it. The tap dancing took place directly in front of
my bedroom.

"*Fabulous!*" my mother shouted. Then, just as he would
stop: "ENCORE!"

Fed up, I opened my door and nearly knocked him
down. "You have to see this!" my mother cried gleefully,
beckoning for me to join her. "Ariel! Come watch—you
can't miss this!"

NOTHING COULD BE missed. Mel the Magician was a
criminal defense lawyer named Mel Sachs, who always wore
a bow tie with his suit. He would store his leather briefcase,
which resembled a doctor's valise, in my bedroom and often

came to my mother's parties after a day in court. My mother would plead with him to perform. "Mel, do some magic!" He would refuse politely, but she would beg, *"Pleeeeaase?"* and it didn't take long for his spirited showmanship to emerge. "Yippee!" she'd exclaim, and then she would silence her guests. They had to stop talking immediately. "Everyone be quiet! Mel is going to do his magic!"

Mel entered my room, without knocking, to prepare. From his bag, alongside legal briefs and files, he took out a deck of cards, coins, colorful balloons, and various other magician's accessories.

"Now I need an assistant," he'd say.

I would decline. Instead, I remain in bed, overhearing the guests' oohs and ahhs and the high-pitched squeaking that comes from twisting a rubber balloon into a dachshund.

THE PIANO WAS on the other side of the wall from my room. Composers would play the score for one of my mother's musicals and someone would sing the lyrics from the songs that she wrote. Performances happened late at night—ten or eleven—and my mother relished the entertainment. I waited it out.

Until I couldn't stand it anymore and then had to confront the ruckus.

"QUIET!" I would shout, bolting up in the dark. "QUIET!"

I was desperate. Exasperated. I needed to sleep. "BE QUIET!" I yelled as loudly as I could, but it wasn't heard.

There was an opera singer in the middle of an aria. There was a violinist playing Mozart. An actor doing a monologue.

"Everybody," I heard my mother cry out, "it's time for the belly dancing!"

I threw off my covers and got out of bed, protesting the disturbance. My mother swore to me that after the belly dancer, the guests would go home. Suddenly Middle Eastern music blasted, and a "famous" belly dancer from Cairo, in a two-piece costume with jangling bells on her bra and chains on her torso, emerged shimmying from out of my mother's bedroom. With finger cymbals striking together to punctuate the dramatic moves, a percussive whirlwind of undulating hips moved around the living room and culminated in a backbend.

I would return to my bed, press my hands over my ears to block out the noise, and plot my escape.

Now I want a quiet life. A home where I am not faced with circumstances that are out of my control. And conflict is not routine. When I need peace, I don't want to have to explain why or bargain for it. I did that throughout my childhood. The need is not trivial. The roots are deep. I am compensating for what was absent. Seeking at the Lost and Found a missing childhood.

22

One of the girls is standing with me in the kitchen as I am making my coffee. I use a French press. Every weekend they help me to plunge. It is a ritual. I marvel at how unremarkable tasks have quietly become significant.

I CALL OUT, "Time to plunge!" and they stop what they are doing to help. One of their little hands goes on top of the knob, then my hand, then another hand, then mine again—until we have a tower of hands resting on top of the plunger. Sometimes they will argue over whose hand will be the one on top, and when that happens, I rearrange the hands so that everyone is satisfied. I count to three and say, "Ready?" They nod. "Plunge!" The coffee grounds are compressed and I declare, "Ta-dah!" All of us remove our hands in unison and hug.

THE OTHER ONE is still asleep. Suddenly she appears in the kitchen with crumpled hair, rubbing the sleep from her eyes. She looks anxious. "What's wrong?" I ask. She says in an injured voice that her sister got out of bed early, and I can see that she feels left out. I reassure her that she hasn't missed anything.

"You were going to plunge without me," she says—as though it has already happened and she is too late.

I don't want her first thoughts of the day to be burdened with worry.

"No, we waited for you," I say with assurance. I point to the French press filled with coffee, the plunger still sticking up in the air. "See?" She nods her head, relieved. She says she has to go to the toilet, and I tell her we'll wait for her to get back. I can tell that she is unsure if this is true and she is torn about what to do. In a voice still unfamiliar to me, a dependable voice that conveys security, I say, "Go to the toilet, we'll wait for you."

She pauses. "You promise?"

I promise, I say. I promise.

EVERY MORNING I hoped that my mother would make an appearance at the breakfast table.

"I want to be woken up for breakfast," she says.

"You promise you'll make it?" I ask.

"I promise."

It was my job to wake her up. I was to knock gently on her door before I opened it and say sweetly, "Good morning, Mommy. I love you."

Instead I say flatly, "Breakfast is ready."

I eat breakfast with Josie and wait.

Just before I am finished, I get up from the table and return to my mother's room. I open the door without knocking and snap, "Breakfast!"

It is, she says, inconsiderate of me to start her day off with such hostility.

EXISTING AS A child was an irritant. I made noise. Shrieks from laughing. Or talking too loud. Toys gave off obnoxious sounds. The game Operation was a torture device. It featured bells, burps, barks, and buzzers. I would sit on the floor of my bedroom with a friend, excited to operate on the bald man with slits in his body that held his plastic organs. The concentration it took to remove his wishbone filled me with pride. I had a steady hand. I'd take a card from the pile—"For $100, take out his spare ribs"—lean in and with exacting precision, try not to touch the sides of the opening with the magnetic tweezers. Because if that happened, it set off the buzzer.

"Josie!!" my mother howled from behind her door. *"I am working!"*

The thickness of the concrete walls between us in the prewar apartment couldn't dull the sound. Josie would appear in the doorway and I would urgently be instructed to play with something else. Something quiet. Reading and drawing were more suitable. Any board game with a noise was an assault on my mother's senses. Operation was retired.

But other games were tricky as well. Trouble had a plastic

bubble. A pop-o-matic that rolls the dice with each pop. I would press down on it with the palm of my hand and when I released my hand, the *pop!* noise it generated was unacceptable. Electronics were out of the question. And dolls that emitted a sound. If a toy or a doll or a game came with batteries, they were removed. Mouse Trap screeched when the plastic cats scooped up the plastic mice on the board. Dice shaken in a cup from Yahtzee were unbearable.

"Are you purposely trying to get on my nerves?" she would remonstrate dramatically, standing in the doorway in a diaphanous dressing gown, exposing her body to my nine-year-old playmate.

I was embarrassed at her nakedness and confused about how I had misbehaved. Most of the time I apologized. But on occasion, I fought back.

"We're just playing," I'd say, with attitude.

"Don't be such a brat. I'm an artist. Do you understand that? Do you have any idea what it means to have to earn a living from being a writer?"

The sounds were making her nervous. I was practicing on the piano. I was whistling too loud. I was a child, existing on the high wire of having to consider her needs above all else. And if I slipped, I would tumble into her rage.

JOSEPHINE WOULD WAKE me up in the mornings so that I could get ready for school. She would open my door, stand with her hands on her hips in my bedroom like a drill sergeant, and announce: "Time to get up! Time to go to school!"

Then she would turn and head for the kitchen to continue making breakfast. I would get out of bed and dress myself in my uniform—the blue-and-white-striped pinafore, navy blue knee socks, and plain white short-sleeved blouse underneath.

In the fall, before school began, Josie took me to visit the special uniform store. It was on a low floor down a poorly lit hallway in a midtown building—not a store exactly, but an office filled with measuring tape and materials. I would be fitted for a new uniform and then would choose from a rack of blouses. All of them buttoned down the front, but some had puffy short sleeves with rounded collars that reminded me of clouds. These were worn in the warmer months. Others were more tailored with clean lines, like a man's oxford shirt, long or short-sleeved, and were available in pale blue, light green, navy blue, or white. Each year the uniform size would increase and it would be hemmed to fall at my kneecap. Josie decided that was an appropriate length. A few weeks before school began, we would go to collect the new uniform and there was a sense of excitement; it was a marker of the passage of time. I was getting taller. I was growing up. I would experience these transformative moments of adolescence with Josie and share with her the anticipation about returning to school—a place I felt safe. I was beginning third grade, fourth grade, fifth grade. A new uniform was something I looked forward to.

As I got older, some of the girls in my class would wear

their uniforms very short—mid-thigh—but those were the girls with long, lean legs they were proud to show off. I never wished to have my uniform shortened, but when I mentioned it once to my mother she was contemptuous. "Why would you want to look like a hooker?"

When I asked her permission to get my ears pierced, she was equally disapproving. This time for my lack of originality. She shot back, "Don't you have enough orifices on your body as it is?"

AFTER COLLECTING THE uniforms, Josie and I would go to Indian Walk on Madison Avenue for new shoes. Indian Walk was aimed at children who went to private schools, and the selection was limited to practical footwear. There was a long single row of chairs stuck together that ran down the center of the store, with seating on both sides and shiny chrome arm rests. And a pervasive scent of clean new leather. The walls were deep bookshelves stacked with cardboard shoeboxes instead of books, and there were several wooden ladders that the salesmen would climb to reach the various sizes on the higher shelves. The shoes were displayed on top of stacked shoeboxes that rose like columns from the well-worn carpeting. Black-and-white lace-up saddle shoes, shiny brown penny loafers, Wallabees in beige suede with the neutral rubber wedge, patent-leather Mary Janes for parties, and the dream shoe: a slip-on tan moccasin. In the springtime, the sandals would be on display: red leather, white leather, all with a thick brassy buckle that dug into the anklebone. But at least your toes would be free.

We would take a number from the ticket dispenser and wait our turn. Someone at the counter who'd worked there for fifty years in a striped shirt with half a dozen pens in the pocket would pull on a string, and *tick*, the number would change. "Who's number fifty-seven?"

"Over here!" I'd call out. Waving my paper ticket to show we were next. Josie and I would be sitting together and one of the shoe salesmen would pull up a footstool with a small slope that resembled a slide. He would sit on the padded part of the stool and then motion for me to extend my foot out and rest it on the slope. When that happened, he reached for the foot-measuring device—a steel contraption that seemed very high tech to my nine-year-old eyes. He would place my foot on the device, my heel snug in the curved metal cup at the bottom, to get the most accurate fit—the length, the width, the arch—it was a meticulous process. He would scribble the measurements down on his notepad before instructing me to switch feet. He would then announce my new size, which I had been eagerly waiting to hear. It was a joyous moment when I discovered my feet had grown.

Josie believed I should wear only sensible shoes. There was no need for a moccasin. No need for a wedge. The Bass penny loafers were the standard purchase, and I would slip on the brand-new pair, and the leather was so stiff and uncreased, I'd slide on the carpet as I strode around testing them out, to the point where I nearly did the splits. Before we left the store, she would reach in her purse and produce two shiny copper pennies for me to place in the empty slots. She'd never forget to give them to me.

Josie remembered these things. She kept track of my appointments at the dentist, the doctor, or the math tutor. She brought me to the after-school activities and the birthday parties of my classmates and we'd shop for their gifts together at Rappaport's Toy Bazaar across the street from 180. It was a family-run store that had been in business for ages. The oak-paneled cases displayed the games and toys, from Silly Putty to pick-up sticks. The store sold everything from bicycles to sporting goods. Items were wrapped in a distinctive polka-dot-covered paper. Sometimes as a treat when my uncle came to visit he would take me there and say, "Pick out whatever you want, champ." I always chose the same thing. A box of Colorforms. This toy was a collection of vinyl adhesive shapes that would stick on a shiny plastic board. The shapes and figures could be arranged to create different scenarios. When I got older, I read that Colorforms was a toy designed to stimulate a child's imagination. But that wasn't why I chose it. My reasons were simple. It was a quiet toy that didn't require another person and could be enjoyed alone.

OUTSIDE OF MY office, the girls are playing with a mouse caught overnight in the rusted metal mousetrap in the kitchen. One of them had the idea to put a peanut in the cage, and it worked. They are elated. They burst into high-pitched delighted laughter and one of them shouts, "Let's put him in the sink and wash him so he doesn't smell bad!" I don't want to know what sink the mouse is going in. They laugh and squeal at piercing volume and enjoy the assorted creatures. There is no apprehension, no fear. They are making a mess. They are banging on instruments. Sometimes they shout. Sometimes they whine. They are seven. They are playing. They are happy.

23

It is 1979 and my mother and I are seated in the of-
fices of Dr. Barry Farkas, an optometrist who has just
examined my eyes.

"Our family has an obsession with going blind," my
mother tells him as he is taking a seat in the chair behind
his desk. He has my file in his hands. "Whatever you say,
whatever you do, please make sure that you do not bring
up any bad news in front of my daughter."

She is instructing him to be cautious with how he speaks
to me. And as she says this in my presence, it causes me to feel
that I am vulnerable. That I am in danger. I have bad vision
and will need a prescription for my nearsightedness. But her
jump to the worst possible conclusion has taken over.

DR. FARKAS AND I are seated in the same office on East
60th Street; over thirty-five years have passed.

"I would never had said anything to an eleven-year-old
girl about her vision," he tells me now in a sturdy voice. I
am forty-four years old and he has remained my eye doctor
throughout the years. A consistency that I appreciate. The
office has been redecorated, but the size of the room and the
view out the window are exactly as they were. On the wall,

there is a framed poster of a Giacometti sculpture. I have seen that poster for so many years and am attached to it in a way that transcends nostalgia. I might feel the same way returning to a neighborhood I had grown up in where there is nothing left standing but a tree, and that tree stands as evidence.

DR. FARKAS'S PRESENCE is avuncular and caring. He calls me *kid* in an affectionate way. "I'm happy for you, kid," he says when I tell him about Mario and the girls.

I've asked him to recall what happened that day in 1979. The day a lifelong fear of going blind was carved out of a routine office visit. I tell him I remember sitting in the office and my mother getting increasingly emotional.

SHE SAYS, "MY father went blind." We are sitting close to each other but in separate chairs in front of Dr. Farkas's desk, and she is holding my hand. She is squeezing it so tight that her rings are pinching my flesh. "I am very worried about the same thing happening to Ariel."

I TELL DR. FARKAS about this memory and add, "I recall that she insisted you reassure me that I wasn't going to go blind."

"Yes," he says softly, "I remember that, too."

I tell him that I recall that her anxiety and terror-stricken manner were scaring me.

He nods. "I would say it was disproportionate to what was happening."

He is a soft-spoken man and his voice is naturally reassuring. But I can tell he is measuring his words.

"I don't remember her being easy to deal with." He pauses. "I'm in a quandary here because I'm not comfortable talking about her. But I can talk about you. I can speak to you about the common experiences when we were all together."

I picture my mother coming into the exam room, contaminating it with her hysteria. "Did I seem as though I was more of the parent?" I ask. "Because I remember telling her it would be okay. I remember reassuring her that I wasn't going blind."

"MOMMY," I SAY, "I'm not going blind. Don't worry."

She starts to cry.

She says, "Your vision is precious. I don't know what I would do if you lost it." She plummets into distress. "My father and I had a secret handshake in case he went blind so that no matter where in the world we were, we would always be able to find each other."

I'm confused. She had said earlier that he was already blind.

She takes my hand and shows me the handshake. It is a

regular handshake, only the pinkie fingers are locked together. "This will be our secret handshake," she says. "So that we will never be apart. Ever."

DR. FARKAS LEANS forward so that both of his elbows are on the desk and his hands fold neatly together. "Well, I didn't have that kind of an insight," he says, referring to my question about being the parent. "I had other concerns. I was trying to give you the right care and do what I do best with an overly concerned and anxious mother in the room. And I thought excessively anxious about blindness in particular."

"The worst-case scenario," I affirm.

"Always."

WHEN IT WAS discovered that I would need glasses, it was as if I'd been diagnosed with terminal cancer. The swirl of panic was in motion. The phone calls. The hypervigilant conversations. Contingency plans. My mother's momentum to seek help was comprehensive. There was no time to waste. I remember her alerting my father in Thailand. "Ariel is going blind," she announced. When I overheard this, I was standing by her side in her bedroom and she passed me the receiver. Hearing his voice from the other side of the world was a comfort. He told me not to worry. "You promise it will be okay?" I asked. He said yes. I believed him.

24

I am sitting with my father at his house in Bali. We have just finished breakfast and have been talking about the past.

"Yes," he says gently, "I remember when you thought you were going blind because your mother told you that you were going blind."

"Do you remember how old I was?"

"Ten or eleven."

"So," I continue, "at eleven I thought I was going blind."

"Your mother *told* you that you were going blind."

He emphasizes this distinction in a pronounced way. To clarify the difference between being told something bad was happening and believing it to be real. Even though at the time it all blurred together.

"Now you're forty-five," he says. His tone is even. Pragmatic. "You understand these things and you're in control of your life. Why can't you just beat those demons and destroy them?"

He sounds genuinely baffled.

"You mean why can't I just get over it."

"Yes." He pauses. It's illogical to him that I would be a thinking person who can't control my thou... you can't get over it, then deal with it in a r...

mature way. Which you're capable of doing with other kinds of decisions."

THE NOVELIST AND I stood in the restaurant, leaning against the long wooden bar, waiting for a table to open up. We'd arrived early—fifteen minutes before our dinner reservation. The hostess had flinched when she said, "I am so sorry the table isn't ready." She looked devastated. "Don't worry," he replied. "It's no problem at all." Southern manners were in full force.

He suggested we have some oysters at the bar. "Sure," I said, why not. I was in Oxford, Mississippi, a place I had never been, having oysters—a food I rarely ate—with an eminent southern novelist whose work championed a life-affirming view.

Being on assignment, specifically for writing a profile, was a mission I enjoyed. To extract and explore another person's inner life meant I could temporarily set aside all the uncertainties and anxieties in my own life. Personal details shared were no less real, but there would be no fallout. Talking in this context was a designated freedom.

But this conversation was different. We had gotten into a genial debate. Is what happened to us what we become? His position toward overcoming misfortunes of the past banked on the virtue of self-discipline. A hardening of one's emotional arteries.

"How we are imprinted is something we are not to be victimized by," he had said. Part of this conversation—his point of view—would later find its way into the interview I was doing.

There was a toughness in his stance that I respected, even though it rattled me. He had a pull-yourself-up-by-your-bootstraps attitude that was intolerant of any alternative.

I had taken a stand, without trying to. And suddenly things had flipped. Rather than reveal something to him, I had revealed something to myself.

"There are," I countered, with a conviction that surged from the tips of my toes, "certain people who have been front-loaded with trauma that shapes who they are. They are disabled. Psychologically. And this does not make them victims. It makes them soldiers."

I thought of people whose limbs were not long enough to step over the mess or swat it away. They tried and failed. Why? Did they lack strength of character? Were they simply not dogged enough?

25

*W*hether abuse of a child is physical, psychological, or sexual, it sets off a ripple of hormonal changes that wire the child's brain to cope with a malevolent world."

DR. MARTIN TEICHER has a sedate manner. I am at ease in his presence. His fingernails have moons of bright white at the tips and he rests his hands, fingertips touching, in a triangle under his chin.

He is the director of a research program at Harvard Medical School and a leading neuroscientist whose focus is on altered brain development in children as a consequence of abuse.

I am seated with him in his office at the McLean Psychiatric Hospital in Belmont, Massachusetts. A few months have passed since Emily's assessment of brain damage and now, in my early forties, I am seeking to get unstuck. He has agreed to let me interview him. I am searching for information. A molecule of logic in an orbit of uncertainty.

"Is my brain damaged?" I ask.

"It's more altered than damaged," Dr. Teicher says.

Over his shoulder, the screen saver on his computer displays an Eagles album cover from his iTunes collection.

"I appreciate the clarity," I say.

Altered feels less severe.

HE TELLS ME that scientists have found connections between children who are psychologically abused and permanent changes in the brain. We are discussing the neurological effects when a child's rational responses are continually invalidated.

"The coping mechanisms that were adaptive in childhood become maladaptive as an adult," he says.

He gives an example.

"When you have an erratic, unpredictable, and aggressive parent, a child will detect signs and know when not to say something or know when to hide, so a threat-detecting sense begins to emerge early on. In the end, it wires the individual to be acutely aware and highly reactive to perceived threats."

HE EXPLAINS THAT the brain is being shaped by these early formative experiences and develops in a way to cope with a world that it believes to be unsafe.

"Children who are exposed to trauma and stressful situations become hypervigilant as adults. So they're always scanning, looking for danger. It's hard to settle down and feel secure if you're wired to always be on your toes. You can wind up with a mismatch if the world you live in is much more benign than your childhood. And so you may be overreacting and over-interpreting stimuli because you're wired in that way."

AS I LISTEN to him describe how consistency, continuity, and routine are the foundation for children to develop a cognitive understanding of trust and security, there is vindication in his proof. My emotionally impaired beliefs have a source.

This information is comforting because it is a real, scientific explanation. Feeling grounded in an uncertain world is not a matter of willpower or *getting over it* in the way one might get over a breakup, a lost job, a death, or an outrage. Adaptive behavior had a price.

"WHEN THE BRAIN is deprived of adequate levels of hormones that are needed for this development, it changes. The cascade of chemicals that are released changes the software of the brain. This is where beliefs, thoughts, and feelings are being formed."

When stress hormones are being released in a developing brain, the physical shape of it changes. These hormones mold the brain to overreact and overrespond. A permanent state of living on high alert.

"But," he adds, "what gets really complicated is that not

everybody who gets exposed to something threatening activates and runs. Sometimes people freeze. Sometimes people shut down. Sometimes people dissociate."

AND WHAT HAPPENS when this software is defective? How does a child who lives with sustained instability and emotionally volatile psychological confusion process it? The collateral damage of living in terror of unpredictable moods?

"A child cannot understand when a mother feels one emotion but expresses another," he says.

It makes sense. I ask, "When the nutrients that are needed to develop trust and security are missing, are they missing for life?"

Dr. Teicher closes his eyes and tilts his head back as he thinks. He doesn't know the answer.

MCLEAN HOSPITAL IS known for its former residents who, with their distinguished madness, gave it a noted reputation. Robert Lowell, Sylvia Plath, Anne Sexton. There are tree-lined paths and red-brick buildings, and the tranquil New England setting resembles an Ivy League campus. It's serene, as I walk around, with raindrops causing the autumn leaves to stick to the soles of my shoes. I eat lunch in the cafeteria near the window, looking out on the hospital grounds, thinking about my altered brain.

If my brain was deprived of adequate levels of hormones

needed and overloaded with unwanted hormones that were too much to handle, then no wonder the wiring went askew. Surely this must have short-circuited my ability to develop a feeling of safety.

I THINK, TOO, about the distinction Dr. Teicher made between *chronic* exposure and a single instance of trauma. He compared this to trees that grow in an extremely windy climate—they will be bent in certain ways. "They've developed in a way that is warped or abnormal—but it's not the same as being hit by lightning."

I AM HUNCHED over my notebook, reading this quote several times: "You try to blunt certain emotions, but your tool isn't a scalpel, it's a sledgehammer. And you're blunting all of them. To protect yourself from feeling the horrible things, you prevent yourself from feeling some of the positive things."

TO COPE, IN childhood, was to be on guard at all times. Sentiment was not to be trusted. Hope would be met with disappointment. This was an operating system that allowed me to function, and it carried over into adulthood. The result was to live a life within brackets. An abbreviated life.

26

I have shown my father a photo of me with the girls. "It's a beautiful photo," he says. And then, because seeing me relaxed is not something that happens often, he looks suddenly wistful. "It's nice to see you like that."

THE GIRLS ARE sensitive little people and their emotions are unfiltered. They express themselves without hesitation, without using their brain first to process. It's purely instinct. One minute they are at ease, playing lovingly with each other, and then a minute later, this can change. The hurt, the rejection, the anger is intense. The disappointment is catastrophic. One might burst into tears and say, "I hate you! I wish you were dead!" and in that instant, the emotion is unregulated by any intellect or understanding of logic. And then it will pass. Maybe in seconds, maybe in minutes. In a calm, steady voice, their father will soothe the one who is angry. He'll lift her up in his arms and take her aside and talk to her and ask what she's upset about. Or sometimes this soothing will come from me.

THE FIRST TIME it happened, I was shocked that the instinct was there and I knew what to do. I kept it to myself. "Sweetheart," I heard myself say, with a gentleness I didn't recognize, "what's going on?" As she started to talk, I listened. It felt like a scene in a movie where the agitated child gets what she needs, and I wondered if maybe that's where I learned what to do.

THEIR FATHER WILL focus on one while I turn my attention to the other, who is sulking—both of them getting the attention they need until they are once again in harmony. Then, without prompting, one of the twins will apologize to the other for being rude.

She says, "Let's never fight again, okay?"

The other one nods. "I'm sorry."

They hug each other and resume playing joyfully.

The girls are allowed to feel what they feel and express this emotion. They are permitted to be angry or to be upset and to cry—without being castigated or instructed to get over it. Even when their anger is directed at their father, he doesn't take it personally. I never say, "Don't be angry"—I only accept and validate their emotions. I let them be who they are. I hear myself talking to them in the way I wish my mother had spoken to me.

ONE OF THE girls says, "I know what you are afraid of."

"What's that?" I ask. We are in the kitchen.

"Spiders!"

"That's true," I say.

She looks at me and smiles. "I knew it."

"I'm afraid of spiders, too," she says.

The other one is facing the fridge. She has been arranging the wooden fish magnets into the shape of a heart. She turns around. "So am I. I'm afraid of spiders, too."

Now they are both looking at me. They are wrinkling their noses and making faces. The expressions are different, but they both transmit disgust.

"No," I say, reminding them of a truth they aren't sure of. "You're not afraid of spiders. You are much braver than I am. Remember the time you caught the spider in the bathtub?"

I have learned to withhold my instinctive reactions in front of them. Mario pointed this out to me when I screamed the first time I saw the giant spider. The spiders in Bali are prehistoric.

"You will make them afraid," he said. "And I don't want that."

He took the girls to remove the spider from the bathroom. He showed them how to do it with a plastic container and a piece of paper that slips underneath until it becomes a lid. He did this with the same stealth that accompanies his confronting the cobras and other assorted creatures that populate the tropics. The rats that come out at night and visit the kitchen.

Mario's nonchalance extends to illness, too. When the girls are sick, there is no panic. No assumption it will soon become fatal. If they have a fever, they lie down with a cold towel and rest. When they cut themselves or fall and bleed there isn't a frenzy. "Poor you," he says in a sympathetic tone and tends to the wound. They do not feel they are in peril. I am in these moments an intrigued spectator. This is how it works, I think, looking on.

27

The times I remember my mother most at peace is when she would stand without moving, unaware of passing time, reading or rereading passages from a book that she'd picked off the shelf. Words were liberation from the frantic world she occupied. She could lose herself temporarily in the sanctuary of the lyricism. Unlike people, words were always enough.

WHEN MY MOTHER would talk about literature or poetry, she was hypnotic. She would explain why the work mattered in such a passionate way that had it not been created, her life would not be worth living. When she was excited about sharing a book, the title was spoken with astonishment. How could such a thing of beauty exist? The poet was majestic. The writer was heroic.

As I got older, I discovered who I was with my writing, and my mother said she was proud of me. Her generosity soared in this department. She was able to transcend her needs, if just momentarily, to support me in a way that gave confidence and strength. She championed my imagination. And this was a kindness I could use. A life raft of encouragement that saved me from the undertow. Because of her, I am a writer.

. . .

THE DINING ROOM at 180 was called the dining-room-library. It was always spoken as one word. Just off the kitchen, the walls had floor-to-ceiling built-in book-shelves and a heavy oak wooden ladder that slid along a brass railing near the top. As a child I climbed the ladder, and when I reached the top shelves, I sneezed because of the dust. I was curious about what was up there. One shelf held a row of Proust, a collection of small olive-green bound books with faded binding. Another shelf was filled with volumes of Shakespeare. These books were leftovers from my mother's days at college. The middle shelves were mostly novels and nonfiction—old paperbacks with yellowing pages that fell out and sprinkled down to the floor if the book was cracked open too far. These relics sat alongside out-of-print hardcovers with austere book jackets. Nabokov's *Lectures on Literature* reminded me of a textbook. An ancient, drab copy of *A Portrait of the Artist as a Young Man*. I picked it up and put it back. Boring! No pictures!

Remarkably, my mother knew where every book was, as though she had an inner compass. The books weren't alphabetized or organized in any particular way, but if she needed to find a certain title, she would move toward it, magnetically pulled to its location.

Each book was a friend who would never let her down. They hung around, waiting patiently, without demands. They never abandoned her. Poems were lovers who would never leave.

·   ·   ·

"OH MY GOD!" My mother would exclaim with the enthusiasm of a schoolgirl. "*You haven't read* The Magic Mountain?" She would stop whatever she was doing and immediately take Thomas Mann's novel off of the shelf. "This book changed my life." I could not last another day without reading *The Magic Mountain*. It was imperative. She held the book in her hands, gazing at it as if she was marveling at the existence of the sea or a mountain—a creation that surpassed human understanding. *Death in Venice. The Sorrows of Young Werther*. She explained why these books moved her—telling the story in a way that captivated me with the richness of their ideas. Talking about books made her feel less alone, I could tell. But there was, too, a subtle message that was never lost. To be cultured and literate was necessary. Essential for being a person of worth. And the contempt for those who didn't abide by this decree was equally severe. The worst thing anyone could be in this world was bourgeois.

ON MY THIRTIETH birthday my mother hands me a hardcover copy of *Humboldt's Gift* by Saul Bellow. The novel is about the life of the poet Delmore Schwartz, whom she knew. She wants me to read *Humboldt's Gift* because it's crucial, and she talks about Saul Bellow. She respects him and holds him in high regard.

When I open the book there is an inscription: "Dear

Ariel, your mother is one of the greatest poets of our time!" It is signed: Saul Bellow.

It's in her handwriting.

"You wrote that," I say.

She giggles in her childlike way. "So what? He thought it."

MY MOTHER WAS always writing. She had to create. It freed her. There was a need to make people feel the things that she felt.

Her disappointment, in later years when no one was interested in her work, was never a deterrent. She would write anyway. As I began to be published, she would say, "I want you to share with me what you're working on." I would tell her about an article I'd written. But I would be wary of giving too many details. "Tell me more about what you're doing—I want to know," she says.

If I mentioned difficulties or frustrations that mirrored her own, she became impatient.

"You don't know how good you have it. No one cares about me anymore."

I AM THIRTY-EIGHT years old and standing in a darkened aisle of the Strand Book Store in New York when I spot a title that I recognize. A collection of mother and daughter poems. I reach for the slim paperback and remove it from the shelf. On the cover it lists some of the writers who have contributed to the collection: Sylvia Plath, Anne Sexton, Adrienne Rich. I see my mother's name. I am proud when I see her name. I know how much it would mean to her that I have discovered this book by accident and realized she was in it. That she was worthy of this company.

I hear in my head the conversation we would have.

"Aren't you proud of your mommy?" she asks.

"Mm-hm."

The parsimonious response displeases me. Because I know how grateful she would be if I told her how I felt. And I wish I could give that to her. I wish I could give that to her and have that be enough. Knowing it won't be, I keep it private.

I turn to the table of contents. The poem is called "Thoughts About My Daughter Before Sleep." I know this poem. She has read it to me before. Many times. It begins: "Ariel, one true miracle of my life," and as I read it, I begin to cry.

BECAUSE HER LOVE was a vapor. It didn't touch, it didn't heal, it didn't soothe. The words on the page weren't compensation for what was missing.

My mother imparted her devotion through words. But words were also weapons. They could embolden and they could destroy. They provided security and ripped it away. She was sensitive to words and she passed that on to me. I inherited the belief that what was spoken could always fix what was broken.

28

Mario doesn't live in world of words. There is an absence of analysis and deconstruction. His feelings are communicated in actions. A discussion is an anathema. He seeks an economy of words—the fewer the better. Intimacy is nonverbal. This is uncomfortable for me. But then, it is also a source of relief.

WHEN I ASK Mario, "How was your day?" he replies with a timeline of what he did. A recitation. Introductory dive, then lunch, then kitesurfing, level two. When he asks, "How was your day?" I begin with "Today I realized" or "Today I felt."

If I ask him, "How do you feel about that?" the response is factual, without scrutinizing or editorializing. He feels good. There was wind. He feels tired. The wind was eighteen knots. If the dive went well, he will demonstrate enthusiasm about the conditions of the water. "There was very good visibility," he says with an appreciative nod. "Very clear."

This gratitude will extend to what he saw. Turtles, sharks, lots of Manta; dazzling descriptions of fish. This is a good day. Sometimes he will add, "I had a German student who told me she is a journalist." A surprising amount of detail. "What kind of journalist?" I'll ask, even though the response is as expected: he didn't inquire. His taciturn nature means he does not ask questions.

HE IS SITTING quietly, staring ahead.

"What are you thinking?" I ask.

"I'm thinking," he begins slowly, and there is a long pause. As if unsure he's ready to disclose his secrets. "It's time to cut the bamboo."

"Why?"

"To create the current in the pond so that the fish will enjoy the flow."

HE IS PACING in front of the fishpond for several minutes and appears perplexed.

"What is it?" I ask.

"I am missing two fish. It's a mystery."

"Why?"

"Because I can't see any casualties."

"What if they were eaten?"

"I would see the leftovers."

WHEN I USE a word that he doesn't understand, he will ask, "What does that mean?" and I become impatient, forgetting that he is Italian. He speaks English fluently, but it isn't his native language. Occasionally, though, there will be a word that is the same in both languages. Oblique, for instance. "Obliquo," he said, nodding. "When someone says something but means something else. If it's oblique, something is hidden."

He knew what that meant.

WE ARE SITTING on the porch, looking out at the sky, which is black with a crescent moon.

"What's your favorite word?" I ask. My head is resting on his shoulder. The breeze moves through the leaves of the Cambodia trees, and they seem to be shivering. Mario doesn't respond. A few seconds pass.

"Did you hear me?"

"Yes."

"And?"

"I'm thinking."

"Okay."

A few more seconds pass.

"My favorite word is . . ." He pauses. "Family."

SOMETIMES I WILL write him a note. I will express myself in a way I couldn't during a conversation. He will read what I've written and comment, "I understand." Two words.

And then one day he said, "You say all these words and write all these words, but it doesn't change how you are."

I PAID ATTENTION to this. Because I can't talk my way out of how I make him feel. I can't alter it with explanations. Or reset with elucidations. So I fight against what feels natural—using words as reparations—because what feels natural is defective.

29

I am nine years old. Before leaving for Thailand that year, a plan was conceived. I had been begging my father to let me stay in Bangkok. Every summer that I spent with him, before I had to return to New York, I would plead, "Daddy, don't make me go back. I want to live with you."

The summer of 1977 was to be the beginning of my new life. Before I left for Thailand that year, we'd arranged an escape plan. That summer I would stay with him. After the years of reports from Rita and from Josie about the "horrors at 180," he had to do something to rescue me. But what could he do? He was a single lawyer living abroad in Southeast Asia and knew it would be impossible to gain custody of me through the legal system. There were many reasons an attempt would be futile. My mother had money. She would hire lawyers to crush him. I was her property. She was a gladiator poised for battle. He was the nail that her mallet would bear down on with such force, he might never get up. She was capable of inventing stories impugning his integrity, loyalty, devotion as a father. The case would go to court and I would have to testify. I would have to choose, and state in her presence that I wanted to live with him. The courts at that time were not inclined to side with a father. Especially an absent father who lived on the other side of the world. No matter how unfit she was as a parent, he knew that when the time came, she would pull it together, streamline her mental state, and perform with credible conviction. She would manipulate, charm, and bully to get her way. She was, as his lawyer had declared during their divorce, "the champion."

HE HAD HIRED an attorney who said he would never win custody. How could he put me through that? When he knew there was no chance the outcome would be in our favor.

But he didn't want me to think he wouldn't try. We decided on a plan. I would write my mother a letter at the end of my stay and explain to her why I wasn't going home. He must have known she would never accept this, that this attempt would be in vain, but maybe not. Maybe he believed if I expressed how much living with him would make me happy, she would relent. She always said she wanted what was best for me. Maybe he believed she meant it. He was willing to try. And that willingness, despite the pressured outcome, was proof that he wanted me with him. That he was not passive, that his desire became an action. This is what mattered. He tried.

I SECRETLY SAID good-bye to my friends. I told them I was going to live with my father with the elephants and the Buddhas. I said good-bye to my dentist and my toys. Josie knew about the furtive plan to stay with my father, and though I don't believe she thought it would work out, she sanctioned the attempt and kept the secret. When I said good-bye to her in June, it was tearful.

In July, I sat down with my father and wrote a letter to my mother. He was living in a house on Soi Phiphat. There was a garden and we sat outside at a white cast-iron table. The letter was a plea to let me live with him. I would go to an international school in Bangkok. I implored her to let me stay in Thailand because that is where I felt happiest. We sent the letter. I wasn't aware of the potential consequences. There was only excitement, optimism, and anticipation for my new life.

I HAD A fever of 103. I remember the thermometer pointing to that number and having a cold compress on my forehead. The ceiling fan was on, stirring the humid air, and outside, there was a monsoon with rain so dense my skin felt clammy. The woman who looked after me when my father was at work—Tootie—was with me. She was from Holland. Tall, slim, with short-cropped gray hair and tanned long arms. She was kind.

When my mother appeared in the room, I thought it was a hallucination. It wasn't. Tootie didn't know what to do. "Ariel is very sick," she said. "You can't move her."

Upon receiving the letter, my mother reacted immediately. She went berserk, called her lawyers, and booked a flight the next day to Bangkok. She had recruited a traveling companion because she couldn't handle the crisis on her own. Salvatore, her tennis pro. She'd paid for his ticket to keep her company and give her support.

Within forty-eight hours, she had shown up. She said, "Your father has tried to kidnap you, but it's not going to work. I'm here to bring you home."

MY MOTHER WAS in my bedroom. My father was not present. My passport was missing. My mother said that my father had stolen it. She arranged for the consul general to issue another passport so that I could leave the country. She was arguing with Salvatore, whom she called "useless" and an "idiot." There was a scene in a hotel lobby, where she hurled obscenities at him; luggage was lost. Who packed my bags when I left Thailand?

THE AFTERSHOCKS CAME years later. The feeling that I will never be free from her. I will never know peace. Her menacing presence will govern my fate. No matter where

I am in the world, there will be no escape. She will track me down, she will not let go.

In Thailand, I had been safe. I had been sheltered. And then yanked, like a weed from the garden, I was gone.

AFTER THAILAND, MY father and I had secret phone calls where we talked freely. Sometimes we were in the middle of having a conversation when suddenly my mother's voice would barge in. "That's a lie!" she'd shout. She'd been listening in on the other extension.

"Did you speak with your father?" my mother often asked. The interrogation was relentless. No, I lied. It was easier than giving her an inventory of what we spoke about and carefully editing out what would anger her. Before Thailand, after Thailand, this is the way it had to be. Managing her feelings was paramount. If she didn't feel abandoned, she would not attack. It was compulsory to assuage her fears. Hearing my voice made her happy, not hearing my voice made her unhappy. If I had a different opinion or a different *feeling*, she felt threatened. Not giving her what she wanted provoked her wrath. There were no limits to how far she would go.

"I have to see you."

· *An Abbreviated Life* ·

· · ·

SHE WILL HARASS others for information about me, have them write to me and tell me she's dying. She's not dying. She will call Interpol and tell them I'm missing. I am not missing.

Now, in Bali, it has been ten months since I've been untethered from my mother. And in this respite, I have been free.

30

Where were you?" I ask my father. I don't want him to feel guilt. He is eighty-five now. We are having lunch at his house and I am asking for details to explain what happened that summer. I am protective of him, as I have always been. He did the best that he could with what he had. My father is thinking. "I was," he begins thoughtfully, and I can tell he is putting it together as he says this, "in America."

"You were in *America*?"

HE DOESN'T REMEMBER my account of what happened. "Memory is selective," he says. He looks away for a few seconds. He is searching. But I am looking for something he can't give. He says in a placid and solemn voice, "At that time, I was not in control. I was not well. Not managing."

For years after it happened, my mother said, "Your father tried to kidnap you and he failed and had a breakdown." That is the story she told.

I ask him to tell me the real story.

What happened when my mother showed up in Thailand?

"I was," my father begins, "in a hospital in America—in

Utica, I believe. I'd had a relapse of hepatitis, which I had initially contracted when I was in the Marines."

He veers off and tells me the story of how he got hepatitis. His face softens.

"Actually, I remember this part quite well. Second Marine Regiment, on cruise duty in the Mediterranean. In the fall of 1953, we put in at Taranto [the Italian naval base in Apulia, southern Italy] for R&R, and we were playing softball. As I ran the bases, I got tired and I remember thinking, 'This is what it's like getting old!' I was twenty-five."

He laughs ruefully and I think about how in the moment when he knew something was wrong, he didn't assume the worst—and still doesn't.

"What I remember are the pleasant memories. The trip we took to the British Virgin Islands."

"It was Virgin Gorda," I say.

"I can still see the beauty of the bay."

WHEN MY MOTHER reclaimed me from Bangkok it was a traumatic time for him, but that's as far as it goes. There is a blackout—emotional amnesia for any negative memory. It's how he coped. The pain and the stress and the strain have been deleted. As if it didn't occur. He remembers uncomplicated, joyful times; sunshine and white sand. The darkness of this memory is mine alone.

31

It wasn't the loudest and scariest explosions that caused the most damage. It wasn't the discernible traumas: the sudden death of my surrogate mother, nor the physical violence I endured—being slapped, punched, kicked, pinched, and attacked during arguments. It wasn't the vile and abusive words that were sprayed over me like an ice-cold sprinkler I couldn't jump out of into the warm dry air.

Nor was it the embarrassment and shame from a cavalcade of scenes. In the apartment. Or in the restaurants. Or in the lobby. On the sidewalk. At my grandmother's house. Or in the car with Donald, driving back from my grandmother's house. Or anywhere, at any time, when she didn't get her way. Nor was it being woken up in the middle of the night by a thunderclap of screams from her debauched and drunken exploits. Not even seeing her arrested and restrained by the police in handcuffs.

What did the real damage was buried beneath the surface. Her denial that these incidents ever occurred and the accusation that I was looking to punish her with my unjustified anger. The erasure of the abuse was worse than the abuse.

. . .

WE ARE NOT calling it brain damage. We are calling it an altered brain. A brain that was denied nutrients such as stability that were needed to feel safe and grounded. Emily believes that a therapy called EMDR (eye movement desensitization and reprocessing) will help me. She says, "Early childhood trauma has a profound effect on your ability to function as an adult."

The consequence of my childhood trauma is a bespoke suit of armor that can't be discarded. Love is unreliable. Joy does not sustain. Good things will go away. I need certainty in an uncertain world, and the tyranny of the past dominates the present.

JUST BEFORE I started EMDR, I had given up the flat in London. My contract with the *Sunday Times Magazine* had ended after ten years, and I found myself back in the apartment in New York. I had lost my family at the magazine, my sense of being a part of something larger than myself. Even though it was professional, it had been mooring. I had no steady income, no escape, and my mother on my doorstep.

I was sinking, steadily and with little resistance. At forty-four years old, I was chest-deep. Extricate myself or be engulfed.

.   .   .

EMILY FEELS THAT by reprocessing some of my earliest experiences and memories, my nervous system will recover. She uses the word *regulate*. It sounds clinical. But this word means the difference between moving forward and being stuck. This inability to regulate makes for a defective operating system. A twisted mess of wires that needs to be untangled. My mother's inability to regulate was out of her control. Is it out of mine, too? Emily has no reservations that EMDR will help me. "You are," she tells me, "still an emotional hostage to the way you were as a child."

I TRUST EMILY, which allows me to defy my innate cynicism about this form of therapy. I research it for weeks. It was developed by Dr. Francine Shapiro in 1987. It was intended for treatment of post-traumatic stress disorders (PTSD). Dr. Shapiro's theory that the experience of trauma results in an overly stimulated part of the brain correlates with what Dr. Teicher said about pathological changes to brain chemistry. I read about brain hemispheres and cortical regions and neural pathways and what happens when cortisol (the stress hormone) excessively floods the amygdala and hippocampus—parts of the brain where thoughts and emotions are formed. I read about bilateral stimulation. And how enlarged amygdalae are linked to childhood anxiety. I read about interrupted attachments when the primary caregiver dies.

. . .

IN EMDR, THE patient focuses on a disturbing memory or thought while undertaking a repetitive series of eye movements. He or she follows a series of blinking lights while listening through headphones to a variety of beeps, all while talking through a memory and exploring the negative beliefs associated with it. The bilateral stimulation from the lights and sound rewire the brain, gradually eliminating the emotional sting from lingering memories. Thoughts and emotions are reprocessed and the patient is healed from the psychological trauma. At least that is the theory.

I'M AFRAID I will suffer a psychotic break.

"You won't," Emily says reassuringly. "You're not a candidate for that."

"How can you be sure?" I ask.

I want guarantees. Nothing bad will happen. I won't lose my mind. I won't be out of control.

She is staring at me with a look that suggests she would roll her eyes if it wasn't unprofessional. She lets out a sigh. I can tell from her aplomb that nothing catastrophic will happen, but I have regressed. You promise? You promise it will be okay? How do you know? The seven-year-old looks down into the lap of my adult body. My arms are listless and my hands rest flat on my upper thighs. After a few seconds, still not looking up, I begin to make a swooshing movement with both of my hands. A deliberate and rhythmic move where I brush off an invisible layer of silt that rests on top of my jeans. Sediment from the erosion of childhood. This silt is resistance to change. I sweep it away. Just like that.

EVERY WEEK FOR nine months I make the trip on the subway to the Upper West Side. Like a migrant carrying around my only possession: a passport of pain.

I walk from the train station to Emily's office. I pass the pharmacy, with expensive face creams in the window. I pass smiling parents on the street, pushing children in strollers, even in the snow and the sleet. I stop for a cold bottle of water on the corner. And enter Emily's building, ready to put things in order.

ON SOME DAYS, this is all that I do: wake up, make coffee, believe it will get better, go to EMDR, believe it won't get better, walk downtown on West End Avenue afterward, thrusting my fists deep into the pockets of my coat, crying. The broad sidewalks are ideal for these tear-soaked extended walks. I try to process the repro- cessing. Passing pedestrians pay no attention to me. I am no one. Just another crying woman wandering in Manhattan.

* * *

THERE ARE TIMES I'll be walking down the street and wonder: What do I look like to other people? Do I look like someone I'd want to talk to? Do I look like I could be Irish? When I visited Dublin, people there thought I was Irish. I have dark hair. I have blue eyes. Why not? I like the feeling of walking around and having a secret. I like that I have something all to myself. I can be standing next to someone on the sidewalk, waiting for the light to change, wondering how it would feel to be hit by a garbage truck. I can think "That's an ugly baby" and smile. Sometimes there will be a sensation, a fracture of the moment, and I will have a wave of understanding how in the absence of learning what was appropriate, I devised my own interpretations. I will walk along thinking about this until it gets dark. Thinking how there are some people who will never be seen or known or found.

EMDR REMINDS ME of a neurological do-over. The trauma—which I don't even recognize as trauma but for me was everyday living—I envisage as dense and intractable ice sculptures on display in my brain. I have maneuvered around these obstacles. The angles are pointed and sharp. These ice sculptures are past events that prevent positive beliefs from getting through. They're on permanent exhibition in the prefrontal cortex and cause conclusions to be drawn and reactions to be had that should not be there.

They don't melt with time or age. And their presence informs how I feel. Now these ice sculptures can be thawed.

I WEAR A hooded sweatshirt to each session so that I can pull the hood up over the headphones. This becomes ritualistic. The sweatshirt functions like a cotton talisman. I sit down on the leather sofa. The lighting in her office is soothing and pleasant. For weeks in advance we have discussed "targets"—negative beliefs associated with traumatic events.

Emily's notepad is full. She flips through the pages on the white legal-size pad and chooses memories where I felt helpless. We banter back and forth about them, and I object to the memories she chooses. The time when Kiki died. The time when my mother came to Thailand. "They're all anecdotes," I say. "I don't feel anything."

Isolating a particular memory seems useless because the trauma wasn't an incident but a state of being. How do you make the feeling of *aloneness* a target memory?

SHE IGNORES MY question and brings out the EMDR "machine." I call it the light saber. A rectangular metal bar sitting on a tripod and resembling a flattened crowbar with small holes dotted along its length, it looks like something that belongs in the bedroom of a teenage boy.

She plugs it in. The holes light up and begin flashing the luminous green of a stoplight. The lights then move in a linear fashion, one hole lighting up at a time. My eyes follow the green light as she works to adjust the speed. Back and forth. Left to right. Right to left. "Slower," I say. "It's going too fast."

She dials it back. Now my eyes adjust.

The headphones are also connected to the machine and there are syncopated beeps as my eyes follow the lights. "The beeping is too loud," I say. She turns down the volume and they become fainter.

The lights are slow and the tones are dim, so we proceed. We have talked about what I want to change. She is trained to do EMDR, and she follows the protocol exactly. I try to delay by asking questions or making witty comments, but she won't have it.

I TAKE A deep breath. My eyes are moving. Emily speaks to me and I am responding. I give an unemotional, detailed observational account of witnessing a violent scene. I am in danger. My fist is clenched so tightly I can feel my nails digging into my palm. I take another breath, my eyes are moving, I am describing a situation where my reality was canceled, and as this happens, my cheeks become flushed and burn with rage. I am powerless. Devoured with a tension that is so intense, there is a lump in my throat and I can't swallow.

"Keep going," I hear her say. "Just a few seconds more."
We stop. I exhale. We start again. Eyes moving left to right.
The sensations are strangulating. Betrayal. Loneliness. Neglect. Panic. I begin to sob. Back then, there was no escape.
We stop. I take a deep breath. We start again. This time as I
describe what happened, the sensation of helplessness is less
powerful. I see my mother for who she is.

THE SESSION ENDS with a final round of installing a
positive feeling to replace the negative ones. My mother
couldn't help herself, but I can. I took care of myself.

The machine is turned off. I feel hollowed out and
tired.

But before I leave the office, Emily wants me to do a
visualization exercise. "Come on," I say, wincing. But it's
part of the protocol, so I reluctantly agree. She tells me to
picture myself somewhere where I feel relaxed. We run
into trouble. I can't come up with anywhere. "Okay," she
says, "somewhere you feel good."

I settle on seeing myself in Bali, because when I have
visited my father there in the past, it's a place in which I
feel relatively at ease.

32

Nearly two years have passed since my EMDR sessions and my days are filled with what I can't imagine. I can't imagine telling the girls to shut up. I can't imagine snapping at them "Stop whining!" even when they are tired and the whining gets on my nerves. I can't bring myself to scold them without considering what to say and my tone of voice. I'll be confused for a few seconds as to what is right. Am I responding to them fairly? I will say, "Please don't shout." And they will stop.

"Are you angry at me?" one of them asks. She looks nervous. "I'm not angry," I reassure her.

I can't imagine telling them stories about my childhood with information that would frighten and confuse them. I make decisions about what's appropriate and filter out what I can share. I share very little. When I mention this to Mario, he says, "That's normal, no?"

I COVER MY mouth so as not to pass on the germs and infect them. That's normal. You don't want to infect your children. You don't want them to feel your pain and your sadness and your anger and your depression. You don't want to expose them to sickness. You don't want them to feel sorry for you. You want to insulate them from your suffering. That is normal. A normal I've never met. Normal is not exposing children to every feeling as it occurs.

THERE IS A sign that hangs on the door of the bathroom. It reads *Family Toilet*, and underneath it has the girls' names and Papa and Ariel allowed. We made the sign with watercolors and Magic Markers; colored it in and drew butterflies and stars.

All of us use the same bathroom and there is no guaranteed privacy. This is new to me. I am sitting on the toilet when the door opens and the little girls walk in. "Hi, Ariel," one of them says sweetly. The other one asks, "What are you doing?"

At that instant, I'm unsure how to answer.

In one week they will turn seven years old. What is the right age to explain what menstruation is? I know they are too young to understand, but I don't want to lie.

"This is something that happens when you grow up," I begin slowly, trying to figure it out as I go along.

They are listening carefully, the way they do when I'm about to tell them a story.

"One day something happens to your body so that you will be able to have a baby."

I stop myself from going on. They've lost interest. They are standing by the sink, where they are playing with a can of shaving cream. One of them pumps a dollop of foam into her tiny hand and turns to me, "Like when we were in Mama's belly."

"Exactly," I say.

I CAN'T IMAGINE wanting these little girls to identify with sorrow. I can't imagine hitting them. Or slapping them across the face. Or kicking them or jerking them or squeezing their arm so tight it leaves a bruise. I can't imagine promising something I don't deliver. I can't imagine accusing them of trying to hurt me or hating me or being jealous. I can't imagine condemning them for not listening to my problems—or spewing words of contempt that shred their fragile self-esteem. I can't imagine ignoring them when they plead for my attention or to be listened to. When they ask a steady stream of questions ("Is the tooth fairy real?" or "Why can we throw peanut shells on the sand and not plastic?" or "Why do flowers smell?" or "Is ketchup healthy?"), I can't imagine ignoring their curiosity. Because they need to be heard, and at that moment, this is more important than anything else. They are hungry for attention. I can't imagine starving them.

THIS IS HOW it is now. These moments, filled to the brim with complicated narratives, are part of my life. And every moment I absorb how much attention they need, I experience how deprived I was. But this awareness of neglect is not a sorrowful feeling or a spasm of self-pity. It is a stunning and lucid clarity of the loss. Every moment I can't imagine is also a moment of remorse, release, and emancipation.

33

After my mother sold a book that she wrote, she bought a Ferrari. It was an impulsive purchase. A fire-engine-red Testarossa convertible. She admired the beauty but it was the speed that she craved. It lived in a garage on East 86th Street. She didn't have a driver's license and never learned how to drive.

Jeff, her laid-back, dope-smoking windsurfing instructor, drove the car. He'd pick her up and they'd take off, flying out of the city, sometimes for days at a time. There is a photograph of her in the passenger seat, hair blowing away from her face, arms straight up in the air. She has a smile that conveys total abandon. She could experience freedom—intermittent happiness—which was deeply felt. But it had no traction. And after a few months the car was gone. She told me she needed to sell it to pay for my school.

ONE WALL OF the dining-room-library was covered with a large Cy Twombly painting. The canvas was tan with streaks of black and gray and splashes of red. My mother adored the painting and I got used to it being part of my everyday life. "This painting is very valuable," she would say. "And one day it will be yours." It was sold.

· · ·

NEXT TO THE painting was my favorite thing in the house. A vintage Charlie Chaplin Mutoscope from the 1930s— the kind of penny arcade machine that looked like a shiny red mailbox on stilts. It was cast iron and fully operational. When a penny was dropped into the slot, I would turn the crank and press my eyes into the viewer. A lightbulb would come on, and then a reel of Charlie Chaplin still photos would fall one at a time in front of the viewer, similar to a flip-book. The faster I turned the crank, the faster the images would fall, creating a sequence of movement. It was like watching a silent movie.

The marquee on top of the machine had a black-and-white picture of Charlie Chaplin leaning on his cane, and the name of the film might have been *Kiss Me Again*. Below the crank was a locked metal drawer; this is where all the pennies would collect. There was no key to unlock it, but I figured out how to open it with a bobby pin. Once a month I would empty it out onto the dining room table. I'd use a glass goldfish bowl and fill it to the brim with pennies. Then I would carry the fishbowl of pennies in my arms to the bank around the corner. I'd hand it over to the bank teller and she'd give me in return several rolls of new copper pennies in stiff cardboard tubes.

No matter how many times I'd seen the Charlie Chaplin movie, I never tired of watching it. It stopped working when one of my mother's dinner guests drunkenly put a quarter in the slot meant for a penny. The quarter jammed in the slot, and my attempts to poke it down with a knife only made it worse. After that, the Charlie Chaplin machine remained in the same place, broken and out of order. But I liked having it around. "This machine is an antique," my mother would say. "One day it will be yours." It was sold.

THROUGHOUT MY LIFE at 180, I listened to my mother's constant refrain about the worth of the apartment. My mother owned it outright, and over the years, it had increased in value. This would only continue, she said, no matter what. It was a major asset. I was instructed to be grateful I had such a beautiful place to live; told to feel lucky I would have it forever. I did not have anxiety about financial security because my mother would reassure me that I would never have to worry. "You're going to inherit a million-dollar apartment," she would say. Under no circumstances would she sell it. "Do you understand?" Yes, I understood. There was a commitment to take care of me financially that accompanied the tremendous theatricality about her money woes. She would sacrifice so I didn't have to.

"You can count on it," she said. The apartment was sold.

34

On the morning of September 11, 2001, I was in my studio apartment in the West Village. The phone call with my mother the night before had gone on for nearly an hour.

"But you *promised me*!" she said, stamping her foot so forcefully, I could hear it hit the floor. She was having a tantrum. A bold, unabashed declaration of disappointment. Life as she knew it was over.

"I didn't promise you," I said, calmly pointing out the truth for the sake of accuracy.

"You did!" Her voice had the agony of a five-year-old denied an ice cream. "You promised you would be there and it's my sixty-fifth birthday today and you are my only child. David has offered to have the party at his apartment, which is five minutes from where you live!" She heaved a sigh of disbelief. "Is it too much to ask that you would show up? I would think you might *care* about making me happy and *want* to be there."

When she got no response to this, she paused. "This is the last birthday party I'm ever having."

. . .

THIS IS THE last birthday party I'm ever having. She was turning forty. This is the last birthday party I'm having. She was forty-five. Forty-six. Forty-seven. The last birthday party was her fiftieth. Her fifty-fifth. Every year it was unquestionably the last birthday party she could afford to have, and every year I would hear her persuade guests to show up.

She would plead: "Judy, you have to come. Everyone else is canceling. No one is going to be here." She would lament: "I have all this food and booze and it's just going to go to waste. You have to make it. Please. *You have to*."

Judy would promise to make it. Then my mother would add, "Make sure to be on time."

Judy would arrive to a living room filled with guests. She was on time. At least sixty people would already be there. Donald, the Goldbergs, James Earl Jones, the lady from the elevator, the tennis pro. I was stationed at the front door as the greeter. Instructed to say, "Please have a drink, my mother will be out soon."

SO WHEN THE phone rang, on the morning of September 11th, I assumed it was my mother again. When I answered, I was relieved to hear my friend's voice on the other end. But he sounded cold.

"Turn on the television," he said. I reached for the remote and stood in front of the screen; I watched as the second plane hit the tower. I did not sit down. My friend, who had been silent on the line, said softly, "Oh my god!" and I gasped as well. I didn't move. The sirens outside the window became increasingly louder; they didn't fade into the distance, as they usually did, but continued to wail and the noise amplified. St. Vincent's Hospital was on my street. Ambulances were arriving at an alarming rate. I heard my friend say, "I'll call you back," and he was gone.

I didn't move from the spot I was in. I couldn't. Standing immobilized in front of the television screen, the cordless phone in my hand; it was a jolt when the phone rang again because I'd forgotten I was still holding on to it. I answered immediately, assuming it was my friend calling back.

My mother says, "I can't believe this is happening."

I tell her, "I'm watching it now."

"It's awful. And David's apartment is downtown." She sounds distraught. "You realize that now no one will come to my birthday party."

35

I arrive home from school and Charlie, the elevator man, is on duty. He has thick, oily black hair that is slicked back so that track marks from the comb are visible. I have known him for all of my twelve-year-old life, and other than to mumble "Good morning" or "Good evening," he has rarely spoken with me. I am the only one in the car and I lean back against the wall, counting the floors as we move upward in silence. We reach the last stop and the elevator jolts to a halt. As he unlatches the metal gate, just before the heavy doors clang open, he says, "None of us like to go to Penthouse G."

WHEN DONALD STOPPED drinking, the scenes with my mother continued, but no matter how much she provoked him, he remained sober and unflappable. He went to a clinic in the Midwest and "dried out." That's how he referred to it. He had a health scare, and when he returned he was devoted to the Pritikin Diet. We would cook oatmeal together, and there was never a time when I didn't want to have him around.

.   .   .

"WE ALL LIVE in a yellow submarine. A yellow submarine! A yellow submarine!" My mother is singing and animated. She is sitting in the front seat of Donald's lemon-yellow Cadillac and I am in the backseat, perched on the divider so that I can see straight ahead. The tan seats smell of leather and the three of us are heading up to Westchester on a Sunday to visit my grandmother in Scarsdale. There is a feeling of normalcy to this outing that puts my mother at ease. With Donald at the wheel, she is calm. He knows the way. He is wearing his "chauffeur's hat," a flat cap of brown corduroy. When we pass by a Kentucky Fried Chicken, Donald talks to me about the "secret recipe" and I ask him questions about Colonel Sanders. He answers me affectionately. As he drives, my mother sits in the passenger seat smoking and talking about herself.

After the day at my grandmother's, I dread the ride back to Manhattan. It gets dark as we approach the city, and there is a moment when my mother's mood shifts and she begins to fixate on what happens when we get home. It is a Sunday night and she doesn't want to be left alone. "I don't want to spend the night by myself!" she shouts. Even though she is with me.

AS I GOT older, Donald and I developed a friendship independent of my mother. There was a feeling of kinship. We had her in common. We always took each other's side no matter what, and this would alternatively amuse or infuriate her. He was generous with his money and gave willingly, but it was his time that I valued the most. He helped me with homework when Josie had her day off. He showed up for my performances at school and on Parents' Day. My friends thought he was my grandfather. And when I did well in school, he was proud of me.

Donald never spoke a bad word to me about my father, and there was a mutual respect. "Donald is a good man," my father would say. He was grateful that Donald was in my life.

FOR THE FIFTEEN years that Donald and my mother were together, off and on as a couple, it was a mystery why Donald put up with the stress and aggravation. No one could understand. He didn't need her. He had his own money. His own life. But in spite of my mother's verbal and physical attacks, he wouldn't desert her. The scenes were predictable, so much so that he became accustomed to them. He was adamant they would never live together, but she never gave up hounding him.

After the apartment at 180 was sold, my mother moved us into a building on Third Avenue directly next door to his. It took her less than five minutes to be in his lobby when he refused to pick up the phone and speak to her.

Sometimes she would have my grandmother call to beg him to forgive her. My grandmother would cry into the phone, "Please, Donald, you know how she is. She can't help herself. She needs you. Don't abandon her."

He would forgive my mother. Was it guilt? Duty? Probably attachment, too. Years later, after he died, I understood that it was me he didn't want to abandon.

IN 2000, DONALD'S obituary ran in the *New York Times.* My mother is mentioned as his "companion of many years." There is a reference to his wicked sense of humor and how he once had a denim jacket made with a heart on the back and his phone number smack in the middle. It notes that my mother, "who lived with him at the time, remembered being less than charmed." I smiled when I read that she lived with him. She had most likely written that part of the obituary herself or supplied information to the reporter. It didn't matter that it wasn't true. In the end, she got her way.

36

"*Mary Poppins!*" my mother exclaims with the enthusiasm of a little girl. She is gleeful. Giddy with anticipation. "It's my favorite!"

In a few days it will be my mother's seventy-fifth birthday, and I have agreed to see a show with her on Broadway. This is the one she has chosen. I've let her know I'm in New York for a brief period before I return to London. She has extracted a promise that I will spend time with her. And she wants to go to the theater. A play or a musical. "Just the two of us."

WHEN MY MOTHER spends time with me, she will frequently bring someone along she wants me to meet. Whom I *have* to meet. "He's heard so much about you," she'll say, referring to this new Very Important Person in her life. Someone she met on the bus. Or in an elevator. Or in line for a brownie during intermission at the ballet. She will have introduced herself in a way that has made them instantly believe their lives will be enriched, personally and professionally, by knowing her. She will teach them. She will help them. They are beguiled by her charm.

I have to meet this person. He is investing in her musical. I have to meet her new best friend. I have to meet her new student. Her new assistant. Her helper. The composer. The nutritionist who has changed her life.

I'll point out to her that we have limited time and I'd rather spend it alone with her. She'll plead with me: "They'll just come to say hello and leave. They really want to meet you—to know you exist!"

My mother will complain to this new best friend about my neglect of her, and the new best friend will sympathize. What a horrible situation. What an insensitive daughter. My mother will push this person to get involved. To advocate on her behalf. She will give out my email address and my phone number, and the call will come. It begins with: "Hi, Ariel, you don't know me, but I met your mother recently and she's asked me to get in touch with you."

But I know the Very Important Person in her life is a transient. Months, often only weeks later, the story will change and the new best friend will be the enemy. The investor was a user. The helper was incompetent. The story will end with: they screwed me over and turned out to be a fraud.

THERE IS A first-grade production of *Mary Poppins* at the Hewitt School, and I have a solo in the song "A Spoonful of Sugar" and have been practicing for weeks.

Rita has arrived at the school auditorium early and Josie sits next to her. They save seats in a row near the front. The floor of the gym is filled with rows of metal stacking chairs facing the stage. The chairs are covered with a hot-pink plastic padding. My grandmother has made the trip in from Scarsdale and sits next to Uncle Jud, my father's brother, who has traveled from upstate New York to be there as well. In the row where they are seated, there is an empty chair saved for my mother.

From the stage I can see out into the audience. I can see the chair with no one in it. It remains empty throughout the performance. Every time I look out, I am hoping to see my mother.

When the show is over, I emerge with my classmates from backstage and I am excited to see the group who are there for me. Rita in particular. I give her a hug.

"Is Mommy here?" I ask.

Mommy is not there. Rita is careful. She does not tell me this but instead says the auditorium is very crowded and my mother might be there but she hasn't seen her yet. She has her camera with her, a Nikon that is on a thick strap around her neck and makes her look like a professional photographer. She is taking many photos. She has several albums on a shelf in her apartment filled with photos of me and my life and the moments we shared. In all of these photos I am smiling and laughing. In some of them I have Mickey Mouse ears on. I am missing my two front teeth. She saves these albums so that my father can see them at a later date.

We head up to the classrooms and I show Rita a globe and point out Bangkok. My mother has been talking about our moving to Bangkok, and I tell Rita about this with excitement. I tell her about this because I believe it to be true.

It will never happen.

A teacher comes into the classroom. "Ariel has a phone call," she says.

My mother is on the phone. She has called to let me know she is running late, but she is on her way. My grandmother walks with me to the lower school principal's office and takes the receiver. "Suzy," she says, "the show is over." I can tell from her clipped tone of voice that my grandmother is furious at my mother for missing the play.

We stand at the exit of the school and wait for my mother to arrive. I am with Josie and my grandmother; Rita has to leave. She departs with my uncle. There are clusters of adults gathered out on the sidewalk, hovering around classmates who have been in the show. The crowd thins out and I am still waiting for my mother to show up. When she does, she bounces out of a cab, flustered and making excuses. When I refuse to greet her with a hug and a kiss, she is wounded. The hoops that she jumped through to get there at all are unappreciated.

SHE LINKS MY arm as we enter the theater on Broadway. She is delighted. "*Mary Poppins!* Goody! I'm so happy! This is the best present in the whole world."

"I'm glad," I say.

"And I want you to give me more than just a few hours."

I need an out.

"There's a chance I might have to meet someone for work," I say.

"You're not going to rush off, are you?"

"No." I reassure her I won't rush off. But afterward, I might have to work.

This is not acceptable.

"You can reschedule. Can you spare an afternoon *and* an evening? Can you be a loving daughter for once and spend a little more than a few minutes with me?" And then, inevitably, "After everything I do for you?"

I give in. Weary from her persistence, I don't want the hassle of combat. That I don't choose to spend time with her is something she could never make sense of. We will spend the afternoon together. "And I don't want you to make other plans," she instructs. I can hear the tension in her breathing subside. My resignation is her victory.

I LOOK AROUND at the audience in the theater for *Mary Poppins*. It appears we are the only adults who do not have children with us. She is humming the melody of "Chim Chim Cher-ee."

Suddenly she begins to limp. "What's going on?" I ask.

"How do you think we got these seats?" she replies with a giggle.

"What if they find out?"

"What if *who* finds out?"

We are being led to our illegitimate seats.

"No one is going to find out. And I do have a bad knee."

She limps down the aisle as we move toward a row very close to the stage.

"You don't think it's wrong?" I ask.

It's a question I should have kept to myself. Of course she doesn't think it's wrong. She is impressed with her moxie. But now she is displeased that I am not equally impressed. She detects my disapproval. And pounces on it.

"Where are your street-smarts?" she asks, sounding incredulous. "I *am* handicapped." She laughs. "Emotionally handicapped."

We have settled into our disabled seating in the orchestra section, the show begins, and she is engaged and full of energy. She sings along to "A Spoonful of Sugar" and leans over frequently to comment at full volume about how she's in heaven.

"These songs are genius!" When there is applause at intermission, she stands up and her enthusiasm is uncontained. "Bravo!" she shouts. "Bravo!"

At the end of the show, she limps to cut the line for the bathroom. Afterward, we are standing in Times Square and there are crowds looking for cabs. I tell her I have to go. "Thank you for spending the day with me," she says.

She is emotional. There are tears in her eyes. "I had the best day ever. Thank you. Where are you going now? Can we go out for coffee?"

I tell her I can't, I have to go. "But you promised the whole day and the day isn't over yet." I tell her again that I can't, that I have to go—but she has already begun to fixate on the next time we will see each other. When? When? She can't let go without a guarantee.

Just then she spots an empty cab. She lunges in front of a man who has been waiting and her voice is filled with urgency as she explains, "Please, would you mind if I take this cab? I have to go to the hospital—it's an emergency."

Without hesitation, he takes a step back. Once in the backseat, she rolls down the window and cheerfully blows me a kiss. "I love you!" she calls out as the cab pulls away. Through the open window she continues shouting, "I love yoooouuu!"

I watch the taxi disappear into the Manhattan traffic until it is no longer visible. I stand still as the crowds of tourists pour out of the theaters. For several minutes, maybe more, I don't move. There is no one I want to call or speak to, and I begin to walk down Broadway. Ten blocks turns into twenty. I keep going until I am able to lift off, holding on to my invisible umbrella, from the feelings of the day. Until I am able to savor the sense of relief and it is no longer heartbreaking.

37

I have never seen my mother do the laundry, make a sandwich, or drive a car. I've never seen my mother in a hardware store. She has never paid her own bills or taxes. She has never served on jury duty or filled out health insurance forms.

She was practical in other areas. She was proud of her ability to get what she wanted, never ashamed with the method, and some of the scams—a word she would never use—were brazenly inventive.

Donald, Josie, my grandmother—they all begged her to use the phone book to look up a number. But she couldn't. She was too impatient. Instead, she would call 411—information—and have them connect the call for the additional charge. As she was always on the phone, the charges mounted. The bills for 411 inquiries were astronomical. Hundreds of dollars.

One day, unwilling to pay the bill, she asked to speak to a supervisor at the phone company. She told them the reason she'd used their service so much is because she was blind. The charges were reversed.

She persuaded people to give her things all the time. Chutzpah won them over. There was a multitude of private lessons. Tap dancing, flying, tennis, in exchange for a promise that went unfulfilled. She was industrious. She bartered—instead of receiving payment for a debt, the florist would get "points" in her latest production.

She would relay these stories and friends would laugh along with her at her originality. She talked her way out of paying for a mink coat by offering the furrier the chance to have his company name on the program in her musical. The musical never happened.

Once after she came out of her bedroom wearing an evening gown, she was complimented on the outfit. "All of my chicest clothing comes from the dry cleaner's mistaken deliveries," she said, laughing.

SOME OF HER misdemeanors were easy to spot. She would take a neighbor's umbrella or a newspaper from outside the front door of their apartment.

"But that doesn't belong to you," I'd say.

"Don't worry about it," she responds blithely. "I'm just borrowing it. I'll put it back."

She never did.

When she removed the flowers from the lobby display and brought them up to the apartment, she shrugged when she had to give them back. "Oh, well." She giggled, handing them over to the doorman. She had an ongoing tab at an Upper East Side restaurant, and when she argued with the owner, after her check bounced, he banned her for life. Eventually, though, she persuaded him to reconsider; she paid off her debt and apologized for the misunderstanding. Her heartfelt defense was endearing. Gliding with the smoothness of an eraser, it wiped away the resentment. Until the next time. And there was always a next time.

MY MOTHER MADE connections any way she could. We lived near the Frank E. Campbell Funeral Chapel, which often had services for show business insiders. Sometimes she would dress in black and attend the memorials of strangers. There, among grieving friends and family, she would extract a phone number of someone in the industry who was a potential investor. Or producer. An important contact. She would and could talk her way into anything.

A friend of hers recalled, "Your mother could sell cigarettes to someone dying of lung cancer." She said this to me with admiration.

AS AN ADULT, I could distinguish her actions as moral transgressions. But as a child, the understanding of right and wrong was murky. I knew lying was wrong, stealing was wrong, and fabricating stories was wrong. Yet when

I called her attention to this, I was told I was too serious. If I scolded her, she would scold me back. No bringing up mommy.

As I grew up, right and wrong became absolute. I needed boundaries; they were sacrosanct. There had to be clarity. Certain lines couldn't be crossed. There could be no unpredictability. No margin for error.

38

I am in seventh grade, and my mother has just called my science teacher a moron. She was defending me. She had been called in for a conference with the head-mistress because I had been misbehaving. I wasn't paying attention. And also, I'd stolen a bladder.

In the science lab, there was a plastic torso used to teach human anatomy. It was named Henry/Henrietta. The science teacher would remove the organs—the liver, the heart, the peach-colored bladder—and pass them around the room so that we could examine the valves and the ventricles. On one occasion, at the end of class, it was time to reassemble the parts, and the teacher looked irri-tated. "Where's the bladder?" he asked. No one moved. A second later the bell rang, we filed out, and it wasn't until after lunch, in the cafeteria, that I was caught. A classmate reported that I'd hidden it in my book bag.

Along with two other girls, I was in trouble for this. We had to meet individually with the headmistress—an unfriendly older woman with a bouffant of gray hair. A meeting with her was a serious occasion, and the three of us sat on the hard wooden bench outside her office, ner-vously awaiting our turn.

·   ·   ·

THE MOTHERS OF my two friends had shown up on time for the appointment and were dressed appropriately. I envied that they looked presentable. My mother frequently referred to one of them as a "socialite whore," and it would enrage her that I didn't share her point of view. Her contempt for the other woman's superficial values, designer clothes, and status-conscious conduct had to be validated.

"What is Irene's talent?" she would ask. "Screwing rich older men?"

Maybe she was right. But I didn't see it that way. I saw Irene as refined. A mommy I would not be embarrassed by.

It wasn't until later that I could appreciate my mother's perspective. When I made up my own mind about what my values were, they did in fact reflect those my mother desired me to have. Not *because* of the demand, but in spite of it.

THE HEADMISTRESS SAT behind a large mahogany desk in front of heavily draped windows overlooking East 74th Street. I sat on the couch in her office and waited with the science teacher for my mother to arrive. I hoped that she wouldn't be coming right from her tennis lesson, wearing her sweatpants, tight perspiration-soaked T-shirt, unshowered. When she showed up, that's what she had on. Her hair was messy and flattened from sweat; her tennis racket was under her arm. She sat down and I could see she was aggravated. Not with me, but with my teacher. Her attitude was

hawkish and her flippancy about my misconduct embarrassed me. She was on my side, but I didn't want her to be.

She blew me a kiss and I looked away. I stared at the
floor. The meeting began, and as the headmistress explained why I was in trouble, my mother glared at the science teacher, her tongue wedged in the side of her cheek,
muttering "uh-huh" curtly and nodding. When he spoke,
she could barely contain her indignation.

"Who are you to say that my daughter is incapable of
paying attention? Who are *you*?" She interrupted him and
he smiled uncomfortably.

"It's okay," I said to her, an attempt to defuse the hostility. "I did misbehave."

"I don't blame her for not paying attention," my mother
continued. "I wouldn't pay attention to you either. You
sound like a bourgeois idiot."

She went on. "Ariel is a kind and wonderful person
who has more to offer than you'll ever have. How dare
you discourage her? Where do you get off insulting other
people's children? How dare you bring me in here and ask
me to listen to you insult my daughter?"

Everyone was silent.

"No, it's my fault," I said softly. But she didn't hear me.
She called him incompetent, and the headmistress looked
on, unsure what to do. Then there was a knock on the
door. It was the cabdriver. My mother had kept the taxi
waiting outside the school and he needed her to pay the
fare.

39

Mario is painting a wall of the bungalow when he says, "What I see is that you keep questioning as a way for you to find out whether the answer changes to see if the person is lying or not. To find out if you can trust. It's a test."

He is cutting the tree high above me when he says, "It makes you happy if you can demonstrate the inconsistency in others."

"Happy is not the right word," I say.

The branches fall down, one by one. He is not even visible. His voice comes from behind a curtain of leaves.

"It's not enough to give you a simple answer. There has to be another question. Then there has to be another question after that."

A LARGE BRANCH tumbles down. I move out of the way. He continues in a calm, laconic manner. I crane my neck back so that I can see him and shield my eyes from the sun with my hand.

"You're not programmed to trust," Mario says. "You're programmed to doubt. The fact that there is the possibility to trust leaves you in an uncomfortable place that you don't want to accept. So you keep doubting and you create stress. And when you create stress in the other person, from never being trusted, it will give you what you're looking for and push them away."

He looks at me with a mixture of sadness and patience.

"You have a roof over your head and people who love you. What more do you want?" he asks.

I stare at him, unable to respond.

WHEN MARIO BREAKS an agreement with me or forgets what he said, I am suddenly barefoot and helpless again, standing at my bedroom door at 180, with a feeling of confusion and futility. It triggers a reaction. To him, an overreaction. But I am walking a tightrope high in the air and the rope is fraying. He has changed the parameters of what I can count on. I am no longer forty-five. I am seven years old. I look to him to soothe me, but he can't. I am responsible for soothing myself. It is no one's fault now but my own.

40

I am waiting for my mother in a Japanese restaurant near my apartment in the Village. I am in my late twenties. I am seated at the table; it is lunchtime. She is late. I look around and wonder: what are all these people doing? They look like people who have plans. People who do things on a Saturday. None of it really matters. Sometimes it can be comforting to think about how nothing matters. It just can't be thought about for too long.

My mother walks into the restaurant and my muscles tighten. There are days she can enter a room and it pulsates with her presence. Whoever she talks to will comment on how healthy she looks and how vibrant. Her audacious laugh and dynamic manner will be on display. But today she is not laughing. Today she does not look vibrant. She looks puffy.

Her psychiatrist had called me as I was walking out the door of my apartment.

"Just so you know," he warned, "she's not doing well. She's very nervous about the holidays."

I'd asked him about hospitalizing her and he said it wouldn't help. He said that after three days she'd be released; she'd talk her way out of it. "She's exceptionally shrewd when she needs to be." He told me she's alienating everyone and that no one wants anything to do with her.

. . .

FROM MY MOTHER'S vacant expression, I size up her mood: she is in an unstable state and I will have to be careful.

She approaches the table and I see people whisper comments about her appearance. Her hair is unbrushed.

She has always overlooked brushing her hair. I would make deals with her before she left the house. She'd be about to walk out the front door and I'd stop her, ask her to wait, and run into her bathroom to get the hairbrush. I'd hand it to her and she'd pass it over her hair absentmindedly. "That's not brushed," I'd say, and make her lean down so I could do it myself. Properly. She'd complain I was making her late, but I didn't care. I wanted her to be groomed.

WE ARE HANDED menus.

"I don't feel well," she tells the waiter. "I have a terribly upset stomach."

He looks at her sympathetically.

"I'm nauseous. My stomach has been upset all day."

The waiter stares blankly.

"What kind of soup do you have?" she asks, refusing to open the menu. "I think I should have something hot, don't you think?"

He tells her there is miso soup and seafood soup and soba noodle soup, but she cuts him off. "I'll have the miso soup." She instructs him to make sure that it's hot. She asks if he thinks it will settle her stomach; he says yes, he thinks so. She asks how long it will take. He says not long. She nods.

I look the waiter right in the eye. "Thank you."

HE WALKS AWAY and I notice my mother's hands. She has on the same rings that she's worn all my life. Rings that dug into me when she squeezed my hand. Will those be my hands? Will those be my rings?

I look at her and say coldly, "You forgot to say please."

"Please," she says.

"Not to me. To the waiter."

She narrows her eyes. "I didn't come here to be lectured by you."

I sink down in the chair. It will be a long lunch.

THE SOUP ARRIVES and her mood improves. She is focusing on the past, reminiscing about previous holiday seasons.

"Do you remember how much fun we had spending New Year's in Lake Tahoe?"

"Kind of. I remember when you got arrested."

She laughs. "Okay, well, except for that year."

When she finds humor in bad behavior, it is a relief.

"Do you remember"—I make sure my tone is light-hearted, not threatening at all—"how Josie used to hit me with a hairbrush?"

I am asking this to thwart her idyllic version of events.

My mother smiles and stifles a laugh. Making fun of this amuses her, so I proceed.

"Do you remember why?" I ask. "I mean, what did I do that was so bad?"

She giggles. "You interrupted me all the time. When I was on the phone, when I was writing." Her eyes become tiny moons as she laughs at the memory. "You were a horrible child."

"But what did I do that was *so* awful? What did I do," I say without a trace of antagonism, "that was so bad I had to be hit with a *hairbrush*?"

My delivery cracks her up. "Are you kidding? You would drive me crazy!" She laughs. "You were such a bratty child."

I force a smile. A few seconds pass.

"What about child abuse?" I ask.

This is the first time I have ever said this, and there is instant regret. Those words shift everything. The flame of playfulness is blown out; from now on, we are in the dark.

"Oh, please," she snaps. "What about *mommy abuse*? No one ever talks about that."

MY MOTHER REACHES for her purse to search for her glasses, which gives her a second to reflect, and it is in this moment that I know everything is about to change. She will take in the hostility implicit in my question. Immediately I try to change the subject—I bring the focus back to her and what she's working on—but it's too late.

"Listen, you had a wonderful, beautiful childhood. You had everything a child could ask for. Do you know how many children would love to have grown up with me as their mother?"

She locates her glasses and puts them on. They are lopsided. "Your problem is, you don't know how lucky you are." Her voice is fierce and intimidating. "You had everything and you never appreciated a goddamn fucking thing. Now I need to talk to you about Christmas. You're spending it with me, I hope. We're going to be together, right?"

This is not a question that permits any answer other than yes. The bullying eviscerates me. She is speaking loudly. She is unaware of the volume of her voice. She leans in, over the table. "You only think of yourself. You. You. You. That's all you care about. Can you think about anyone other than yourself? Can you think about me for once? What about me? Have you ever considered that I might be alone and that you're my family? Did you think about that?"

"Uh-huh."

My mother stares at me, squinting her eyes in attack mode.

I stare back at her. I am descending deep within myself. All she needed was a yes—an agreement to spend Christmas with her. I know her needs: to feel I am not rejecting her; that I *want* to spend time with her. But what I need is for her not to expect that of me.

. . .

THE UNRAVELING BEGINS. A pyroclastic cloud of super-heated, scathing words that spew out and engulf me. Until I am gone. Until I become unrecognizable.

"I'm sorry that you're so self-involved that you can't give a shit about anyone else's problems."

I say nothing.

"You despise me." She spits tiny knobs of saliva. "You're just a selfish, ungrateful bitch."

I sit back, anticipating how it will go on, as it has so many times before, with no conclusion, no final word. No satisfactory end. But I sit quietly, not responding, because I brought it on myself. I look down into my bowl of cold miso soup.

"What do you want me to say?" I ask, trying to deactivate the escalating scene.

"I'd like you to say that you love me. That you want to be with me. I want to feel as though I have a daughter who cares about me. Who gives a fuck. I want to feel I have a friend. A family. That I'm not alone in this world. I want to see you. I want to spend time with you. I want you to act like a compassionate human being for once."

AS SHE SAYS these things, I know there is no reasoning with her. If I tell her I love her, it might reassure her. It might calm her down. But I can't say it. Instead I say, "I have to go." And I get up and attempt to leave.

This is a mistake. It ignites an explosive fury. I am leaving her forever, writing her off, never to return.

"Don't you *dare* walk out on me!" She pushes back her chair and leaps up from the table. She thrusts her body forward to prevent me from leaving, but I am no longer someone who can tolerate the tantrum. I am a block of steel, moving robotically, blind to the stares of the other people in the restaurant who have stopped chewing their food and ceased talking. I ignore the weight of her obstructing me. She stands directly in front of me to hold me back, but I shove her off because my adrenaline is pumping in full force and I can escape. I rush out of the restaurant. She immediately follows me into the street, and in this instant I am aware that this sudden outburst has meant no one has paid the bill.

PEOPLE ON THE sidewalk are watching. I feel their gaze on me. Their wide-eyed, openmouthed, stand-in-place-without-moving stares. Mind your own business! Haven't you ever seen an out-of-control woman in public before?

"Go ahead!" she screams at me. Her face has turned red, almost purple. "Call the police! Call the police on your mother!"

She has crossed over. In this state, there's no reaching her. No reasoning. There's nothing I can say that will make her stop. I turn and walk briskly away, but she chases after me. She catches up to me, grabs hold of my arm, snaps me around.

"Let go of me," I say, staring into her eyes. My voice is concave. Is that my voice? I don't recognize it. She is gripping me and I pry her fingers off my arm, bending them back so far, I worry they'll break. I don't want to harm her. This is a spectacle, and I hope no one I know will pass by. But then I don't care. Let them see.

I AM OLDER now, stronger; I can walk faster than she can. I have underestimated my physical strength, so I break away. There is a handprint on my arm from her trying to hold on to me. I hear her cry out, "Ariel! Wait! Don't leave me, please. I need you! Don't leave me. Please. I love you, don't walk away. Don't leave me! You're all that I have."

I pretend not to know who she is calling to. She yells out my name, but I don't turn around. I feel a piercing ache in my throat. She is winded and can't run after me. She stands on the sidewalk, sobbing and out of breath. I turn around, worried. Is she far behind? Is she okay?

She has given up chasing me and is leaning with one hand against a tree, panting. She looks frightened and desperate and helpless and I see her abandoned. A little girl.

"Please, I need you." Tears roll out of her eyes. "Don't leave me like this. I need help."

I pick up my pace, walking away from this person, my mother. No one has to know. I get away as fast as I can, leaving spectators to wonder.

.   .   .

I AM AFRAID to go home. She could be there waiting for me. I go to a friend's house instead. I tell her about the incident, show her the handprint on my upper arm.

"What provoked it?" she asks.

"She was making a scene and I tried to leave."

She hands me a glass of water. I take a sip.

A few seconds pass.

"That's another restaurant I can't go back to," I say.

My friend nods. "From now on, only meet her in places you don't care about returning to."

I AM ON the subway heading back to my apartment. People have just left work. They're everywhere. Don't look at me. Don't talk to me. Don't try to sell me something. Don't ask how it's going. Or give me tips. Go to the gym! Volunteer! Check out the Chinese masters at the Met! It won't help. I am simmering silently. The subway is good for that. I feel anonymous.

When I get back to my building, the bouquet of flowers is waiting. There is also a typed note and several messages on my answering machine. How sorry she is. How horrible she feels and how she promises it will never happen again. She didn't mean to act out, she didn't mean to hurt me, my friendship means everything to her. She says she is behind me with all of her love and all her support. I know that she is. This is the pattern.

SECONDS AFTER I'VE put the roses in water, my grand-mother calls.

"Talk to her, please. I can't take her—she's killing me."

"What do you want me to do?"

"Speak with her. She's worried you'll never speak to her again. Tell her that's not true. You can't do that to her. Talk to her—she loves you more than anyone. She's calling me nonstop, she's hysterical, she says she's going to kill herself."

"She's not going to kill herself," I say.

"She wants me to take a train into the city and be with her, but I can't. I'm not well. But I'm afraid of what she will do. Do it for me. Please." She begs. "Talk to her. She's got to lay off, she's making me sick. I'm too old. I can't take it."

"All right," I say, "I'll call her."

"Call her right now."

"I'll call her soon."

"Call her when we hang up."

"All right," I snap. But then I feel bad, so I say it again softly. "All right."

"She loves you. You're all she's got in this world. She can't stand it when you're angry with her."

I can hear my grandmother crying. I don't say a word and she blows her nose before repeating herself. Begging me to make amends. "You know she doesn't mean it. She can't help herself."

"I know."

·   ·   ·

WE HANG UP and I think of the three generations. I am alone in my apartment downtown imagining my mother alone in her apartment uptown waiting for my grandmother to call from her kitchen in Westchester, reassuring her that a phone call from me is on the way. And I think about how my mother must have reminded my grandmother what a rotten mother *she* was and how she ruined my mother's life, and as I think about this, I pick up the phone and make the call because I don't want my mother to suffer. I don't want to punish her. I tell her everything is okay and I'm not upset. And when she asks if I forgive her I say yes, without thinking about if I do or not.

I POUR SOME ginger ale into a glass. Then I sit down at the table that I always sit at in the chair that I always sit in, and stare at the glass. It is a glass I have been drinking out of for years. Will I have this glass when I'm thirty? I get up and walk into the kitchen. I cut off a slice of a pear using a knife that I bought at the hardware store because I liked the serrated edge. It's not a good knife—there is rust near the handle and it doesn't cut very well. I stare at the knife. Will I be using this knife to cut fruit when I'm forty? I leave the kitchen and stand in the middle of my apartment. I look around. Will this be the couch that I lie on when I'm fifty?

41

The girls are in the backseat, talking about making lemon juice. I am in the front seat and Mario is driving. The sun is streaming in like a laser and the windows are open. We have just been to the local supermarket and are heading home with the groceries. There is a feeling of contentment.

Later that day, when Mario is driving the girls back to their mother, I ride my bicycle at dusk to the pool for a swim. I think about having gone food shopping with him and the girls and how we pushed the metal cart with the shaky wheels and bought harumanis mangoes and cheap pasta and I smiled when he put two jars of Smucker's jam in the cart because he was allowing himself to enjoy something "fancy." The girls were having fun, grabbing my hand, pulling me this way and that as I picked tiny pieces of dried grass out of their hair left over from swinging on the tree. We discovered the imported cottage cheese had come in, and I'd been waiting for weeks for this extravagance.

"Papa!" they shout. "Cottage cheese!" Everyone smiled. I thought about how we celebrate the moments that improve our lives: going out to dinner when the Wi-Fi gets turned back on, or the fish pump is repaired, or when papaya man brings over a fresh papaya pulled from a tree in the banana field.

How ordinary it must have seemed to anyone looking on—a family filling a shopping cart with groceries—but for me, it was extraordinary. Having lived alone for as long as I did with an empty fridge, buying single rolls of toilet paper, never purchasing more than two yogurts at a time, I would look on with envy at families in the supermarket who bought six rolls of toilet paper at once and think: that will never be me.

I HAD NEVER envied colleagues who won awards or friends who purchased new things; and when I won awards or purchased new things, I felt a vague emptiness because it never seemed that it mattered. The material gains, the professional accomplishments—there was never a sense of *this counts*.

This was confirmed when I took in the residual joy from our trip to the supermarket. I felt overwhelmed with excitement to share my appreciation of the day.

I finished my swim and rode my bicycle home. My senses were tingling and I saw the variations of green in the trees and the shifting light in the sky. I heard the acceleration of the motorbike as it passed me by and I felt the warm tropical air on my skin. I smelled the fish that was being grilled on the side of the road.

Later that night, I told Mario how much I had enjoyed the day. And as I spoke the word *meaningful*, it was bittersweet because I didn't believe the word would accurately convey the depth of my feelings. When I open the fridge, there are mangoes. But I don't see mangoes, I see progress.

I HAVE NEVER been to a supermarket with my mother. Groceries were ordered over the phone from Venice Market on Lexington Avenue. The number was written in pen on the wall near the rotary phone in the kitchen, and in the mornings my mother would stand, sometimes naked, and order what she needed that night for her dinner party. She would use a chopstick to dial the number so that she didn't break off one of her long red fingernails. Often there would be loud arguing with the manager of the market because she had neglected to pay the bill for the money she owed and they would cut her off.

"I am your best customer!" she would shout. "This is offensive! You will get paid, just deliver the food and I'll write you a check!" It was an ongoing drama. They would deliver the food and the check would bounce.

She switched markets. Venice Market was replaced with Rosedale, but then the same thing would happen with them and she'd ask forgiveness and apologize to the manager at Venice. She'd go to the hair salon, and after she had her hair dyed and was dressed in a glamorous outfit, she'd hand-deliver a signed book and promise never to bounce another check. Things were back on track. The groceries would be delivered, she would be at ease, her spirits would lift, and her guests at the dinner party would have lamb chops. I could relax and go to school.

ONE DAY I return home from school to a catastrophe.

"Josie," my mother is crying, "has ruined my life." She is standing in the kitchen, rotating the spindle on her Rolodex, desperately searching for a card.

Josie couldn't stand that my mother wrote phone numbers down on the wall. So she took it upon herself to use bleach to make her point. She scrubbed away all of the numbers written in ink and erased the ones written in pencil. My mother's contacts were gone. Forever. She couldn't replace them.

Only she did. A week later, the phone numbers had returned. On the wall, scrawled in messy handwriting, exactly as they were before.

MARIO SENDS ME a text message after work. "I don't feel like talking, discussing, or answering any more questions." I call him and he answers the phone to let me know he is eating dinner by himself.

I don't understand this mood—did his message of not wanting to talk mean not at all? I try to speak to him, but every sentence is a bullet.

"I just want a rest." His words are pointed and his tone is sharp. The more I say, the more he feels disrespected.

But my need for communication is only intensified by his need for withdrawal.

He comes home and goes to a different bungalow, closes the door, and draws the curtains. I am shut out. When I try to enter, I discover it's locked.

"You locked me out?" I speak this into the glass windowpane that separates us.

"No," he calls out from the other side of the door, "I locked myself in."

I LEAVE MARIO alone and return to our room, trying to tolerate the silence. I pace. I think of Gunung Agung, a volcano on the island that dominates the area and influences the climate. It is still active. There is a deep crater, and occasionally it breathes out smoke and ash. The last time it erupted was four years before I was born, and for some reason, this reminds me of my mother giving birth. Throughout my childhood I was threatened with her lava consuming me as I ran as fast as I could, trying to stay ahead of being smothered. Lava love at my heels. It would swallow me up and freeze me in time. I would never be unstuck.

BUT I DID break free. I am here now, in Bali, and I must learn to control the impulses that will destroy the loving climate I thrive in, one that I have fought hard to achieve.

I have the scary feeling of not knowing what will happen. The tiniest rupture feels like a chasm. It is not about the moment; it is forty-five years of history, and I want to know the future is secure. I just want I just need I just I just. I let it go. And I, in spite of my need to be reassured, focus instead on the good feelings. I trust, which is so hard to come by, that it will be okay. That I will be okay. No matter what.

42

Nearly a year has gone by and I haven't called my mother. She does not know where I am and I've moved our communication to email only, with the promise that I will respond.

I stare at an email that has arrived—sent from Helena, a "former student" of my mother's who can work a computer. She has been recruited to take dictation. I read my mother's words typed by Helena.

My mother wonders whether she will ever hear from me. In the face of my rejection, she can't write, her self-esteem is plummeting, and she can no longer be a happy person. She begs me for at least a few sentences on a routine basis. They would restore her life, she promises. Without knowing where I am, she can't function. She is sure I don't want to cause her such pain—so she says—but it is impossible for her to continue without knowing how to reach me, what I am thinking, or having some communication. She beseeches me to find it within me to answer her, to get in touch. Without it, she is crippled emotionally. It would take away her pain and it is, she says, the decent thing to do.

. . .

I IMAGINE THAT if someone were to see this, they would think what a horrible daughter I must be. Heartless, as my mother says. Indecent. But disconnecting is something that is necessary or I will be devoured. It is her or me—and I choose me. There is no middle ground. And slowly I discover that I am able to ignore these emails without fear of retribution. I shrug off the frantic nature, the cries for help, the pleas to stay close. There will be people who see this as insensitive or even unkind. I can accept that. There is nothing I miss.

"DO YOU MISS me?" my mother asks. "Do you love me?" There was no answer other than yes.

IN THE MIDDLE of the night, I wake up from a dream. I sit up in the bed, breathless and soaked with sweat. I can feel my chest rise and fall with the depth of my breath. The dream took place at 180. Most of my dreams are set there. I am in the apartment, usually in my childhood bedroom, and my mother is looking as she did when I was a child; she doesn't age. When I wake up, I remember it for an instant, and then it's gone. The sensation remains. The emotions are as they were then without time or intellect to mitigate them. I am frightened. In the dream I am hiding or panicking or twisting and turning the doorknob of a door that won't open.

I often bolt upright and shout a word so loudly it awakens me. "STOP!" I have rarely woken up from a dream without feeling grateful it was over. If I do remember a dream, it is a dream I have escaped from and have no desire to return to. It's always, thankfully, *just a dream*. If I have pleasant dreams, I lack the ability to recall them. When I go to bed, what I wish for is a sleep without dreams.

Mario, half asleep, asks, "Are you okay?"

I say, "Yeah, I had a bad dream."

He says, "Me, I dream of fishing and I caught a pompano." He rolls over and mutters, "But there was no room in the freezer."

In the morning, the first thing he says is "Non faccio per vantarmi ma oggi è una bellisima giornata."

"What does that mean?" I ask.

"I don't want to brag, but today is a very beautiful day."

I HAVE DECIDED to call my mother at an appointed time, and at first she is overjoyed and grateful to hear from me. "I had no idea what happened to you, no idea where you were. Don't you think I was worried?"

"I'm fine," I say. Addressing a concern I don't feel is about me.

"Where are you?"

"I'm not going to tell you."

I have never said this before. She doesn't take it well.

"Well, I called Interpol looking for you."

"Interpol?" I snort. "You're not serious."

"I am," she says.

"What did you tell them?"

"I said my daughter was missing."

Because Interpol—the International Criminal Police Organization that hunts down terrorists, drug traffickers, people being sought for war crimes or for smuggling children for sex slavery or who have committed genocide—*this* is the organization to call when a daughter wants to have time off from her mother. Perhaps she feels it falls under crimes against humanity.

"I'm not missing," I tell her.

I say this soberly and with a declaration of independence she doesn't hear.

She moves on. "Is there any possibility you can live in New York? Would you like to?" Her attempt to get me to commit to her causes an immediate panic, and I am tense.

My voice is clipped. "I don't know."

"I would love you to. I'm old. And I miss you. I'd like to see you as much as I can. I love you more than any words can say. You're always in my heart. I'm so proud of you, Ariel. I'm so lucky to be your mother."

"Thank you," I say. And then because she needs to hear it, "Love to you, too."

"You're the greatest thing that ever happened to me."

"Okay," I say. "I'll speak to you soon."

"Do you love me?"

"Yes."

"Tell me."

"I just said, 'Love to you, too.'"

She laughs off the remoteness. She doesn't want to push me away. "You're a character. Can I tell you I had a dream last night about Martin Scorsese? Are you ever in touch with him?"

"No. I'm not in touch with anyone."

"Well, you're in touch with your muse."

"I have to go."

"I just want to tell you as long as you're in touch with yourself, that's most important."

"Okay. I have to go."

"I love you." She makes smacking kissing sounds into the phone. "I love you so much. Thank you so much for making my day happy."

HER CHILDLIKE MANNER plunders my heart. And I feel, in spite of my rage, guilty. Because she can't help herself. And she has no idea of the effect it has on those she loves. For so long I was imprisoned by her moods and her threats and her whims. Believing if I didn't give in, she would suffer. I was responsible for her suffering. There were days I was made of paper and days I was made of steel.

"ALL I WANT is for you to be happy," she says before we hang up.

What I need to be happy is to be free. She doesn't want that.

NOW WHEN I hear "You're my reason to live," I don't feel beholden to those words. I don't have to give in to the control. Time off has been a rebirth. The guilt and shame of being responsible for her are fading.

43

"I met your mother," he says, beginning cautiously. I look at him and nod. I will discover nothing new. The scenario is familiar. A stranger has had an experience with my mother, and I steel myself for the story he will tell. I will not show embarrassment. I will not reveal shame. My discomfort will remain private. I will sit listening quietly, and the anger that I feel from being put in this position will recede. I will monitor my response so as not to expose my humiliation. To do that would be unprofessional. We are seated in his office. It is a setting that is in my world, my professional world.

I KNOW THIS story before it's told. The cadence will differ. The details will be new. The manner in which it's told will display scorn or pity or intolerance or disbelief. If it's scorn, I will feel protective of her. I will keep it to myself and absorb the shrapnel of her actions. I will not flinch.

There is a kindness in his voice. This is a relief. He does not sound alarmed. He tells the story in a placid way that suggests he has had experience with this kind of behavior. Without having met him before, we already have a bond.

"She called me out of the blue." He took the call, he

says, because she knew his father. He doesn't have to continue because I know where it will go. She will use this connection to seize on his sentiments. I don't know to what degree or how involved he will have become before he figures this out. But there is nothing he will say that will surprise me.

He continues. "And after speaking with her for a while, I went to her apartment."

This surprises me. Not that she asked, but that he went. I am surprised by the responses she is able to elicit. That people, emotionally intelligent and rational people, can't see through the charm. But why would they? They don't get it. Until they get it.

The visits were at first, he says, interesting. She told him stories that he appreciated. They included his father. But after a few visits, he learned that her sense of entitlement was unreasonable. She expected more time from him than he gave to his friends. To his children. He let her know this wasn't possible. She said she understood.

She went away. He got back to his life. There was a lull.

SHE CALLED HIM again. He felt an obligation. He wasn't sure why. She told him she was all alone. She complained about her daughter not wanting to see her. Her only child. Whom she has always supported. She rhapsodized about her daughter. How brilliant she was. She suggested they get married.

. . .

WHEN HE TOLD me this, I laughed slightly to minimize the awkwardness. I dismissed it as a harmless cultural cliché—the Jewish mother who wants her daughter to be married.

He continued. When he told her he was not available to see her, she persisted. He is a caring person, and rejecting her had begun to feel uncharitable. This part of the story bothered me. Because he had succumbed to the manipulation. I felt impatient with his kindness because I knew it would be exploited. But then I appreciated his kindness, too. Because she needed it.

The story ends with her locating his home number and calling him there. He began screening his calls at the office.

He'd known her one month.

WHEN I WAS in my early thirties I got a phone call from my mother's cousin. My mother had been out of contact with me for several days. This would happen from time to time when she was preoccupied with her life, things were going well for her, and she didn't need me. I was off duty. These interludes were cherished while they lasted.

My mother's cousin told me in a matter-of-fact manner, "Your mother was arrested."

Her boyfriend's mother lived in Westchester. My mother had shown up at her house after the boyfriend had broken up with her.

"Your mother pulled one of her fits on the lawn," the cousin said. She was trying to find him. He didn't want to be found. She tracked down where his mother lived. It was an ambush. His mother didn't want to let her in. My mother was out of control. Broke a window. His mother had a heart condition and the stress was too much. Paramedics came and took her to the hospital. Charges were filed. My grandmother, who was frail and not in good health, had to pay thousands of dollars to the attorney to keep my mother out of jail.

After that, my mother stayed at my grandmother's house in Scarsdale to regroup. That's why I hadn't heard from her.

SHOCK WAS NO longer a part of my life. When I heard the stories about my mother's behavior, the trouble she was in, the damage she had caused, what I felt was relief. Not to have been there. Concern was absent. Sadness was dismissed. Normal emotions had been extinguished by years of experience. Move on. This is what I tell myself.

"HOW DID MY mother get to Westchester?"

This was the only question I asked.

Because my mother didn't drive. And I couldn't imagine that in her highly agitated state she would be composed enough to navigate train schedules. I couldn't see her waiting on the platform.

"She probably took a taxi," the cousin said.

After the arrest, her three half-siblings stopped speaking to her for a while because of what she put Grandma through. One of them never spoke to her again. She felt they abandoned her. She blames what happened on the medication she was taking at the time.

THE NEW MEDICATION made her crazy. That was the reason. The Optifast liquid diet for a month made her lose her mind. That was the reason. It was the diet pills. They were speed. It was never her fault. And when it was, it was worse. The lucid moments were lethal.

"I'm sick," she would say. "I need help." These heartfelt admissions would draw me in. The self-awareness was convincing. "I am not well. I know that. I've been a terrible mother." The confessions were like a narcotic. They smoothed over the pain. Acknowledgment was an anti-inflammatory. The salve that always wore off. But the need to believe it would work remained.

IT WAS HER mother's fault for ignoring her. Her father's fault for forsaking her. It was my fault for not making her happy. She deserves to be happy after all she's done for me.

I must show her compassion. It must be executed in the ways she demands. If I challenged the sickness or expressed hostility, I would suffer more than if I stayed silent.

"How dare you say that to me? I'm not the one who's sick. You're the one who's sick. You need help. Do you know that? You're a sick individual."

"I'm not sick, you are—you admitted it!"

These confrontations were unwinnable.

THE CUMULATIVE EFFECT was for me to hide. To hide is to exist.

WHEN I WAS fifteen, we took a trip to Greece on a summer break. A friend of mine from high school joined us. The first night in Mykonos, my mother took a nap and the friend and I went out. When we returned, my mother was hysterical. A legitimate concern (a worried mother) had become an apocalyptic event. I knew how to calm her down, but my friend wasn't trained. When my mother called her a bitch or a slut, she fought back. I tried to stop her, but I couldn't. She just took off. She grabbed her passport and disappeared. But I was stuck. We continued on to Crete without my friend. I didn't know what happened to her. She was there and then she was gone. My mother told me we were better off without her. Somehow my friend found her way back to New York City. When I began school again in the fall, she had told everyone in my class what had happened.

"See?" my mother said. "I told you that girl was a bitch." This pacified the humiliation. She was on my side. That's how it felt.

She would protect me from the mayhem she had created.

DURING ARGUMENTS AND conflict, there was never a voluntary ending. No "End of discussion" or "That's it, we're done." The end would come only on her terms. When the person she was engaged with was so worn down and beleaguered, they would relent and give in to whatever she was demanding. A plan. Or a time. Or an answer that was satisfactory. Persistence was a wrecking ball.

But sometimes her need was purely for conflict. And when that happened, it was not about extracting something absolute. A time, a place, an answer would be given, but it wouldn't be enough. There would be something deeper, more urgent, more important that had to be addressed. Her stamina in the pursuit was as vigorous as her ability to recover. Her tolerance for conflict stretched indefinitely without ever snapping.

WHEN SHE SAT on top of me and held me down, straddling me to keep me from leaving her, I knew when to become limp and resist so that I could break loose. I knew when to give in because to respond in a rational manner was in vain. The fighting nature I have is from her. Anger was my armor. Defiance was my shield. She could never imagine she supplied the weapons that would be used against her. To protect myself. But she passed on an imperative to survive. To survive was to withhold. To pull back was mandatory. There was always a system in place.

IN MY TWENTIES, I continued to hide by screening my calls. I would tell her, "I don't feel like talking." That statement wasn't recognized. I wish I could have said, "Let's talk when we feel like it." That would have been a luxury. A pleasure. But it wasn't possible. She had to have set plans. She needed an outcome that soothed her anxiety.

Denying her this was a problem. I agreed to meet once a week. Having a fixed date was a solution. During these lunches, I would be careful not to disclose details of my life that she would store in her memory. Sometimes I would slip up. I would reveal what I was doing—with someone else—and she would feel left out.

"Why don't you include me?"

I would have to evade the question with a dexterity that didn't injure her.

There was the cross-examination.

"Where are you going?" she asks. It sounds like an accusation.

"I'm having dinner with a friend."

"Oh, really." Her voice goes up an octave. "Who?"

"What does it matter?"

"I want to know you. I want to know your life."

Wearily I respond. "Kelly."

"I see." There is no interest in how I know Kelly or who Kelly is.

She asks, "How is it that you have time for Kelly and no time for me?"

WHEN SHE WOULD make the comparisons, which she did often, to other mother-daughter relationships, I stayed silent.

"Why can't we have a relationship like Roz and her daughter? Her daughter invites her to things all the time. They're best friends. How do you think that makes me feel? It makes me so sad you don't want to spend time with me. People ask me why my daughter will only see me once a week. It's embarrassing."

MEETING HER ONCE a week became impossible when I began working in London. At that point, in my late thirties, for the first time I became unreachable because I had a phone number that I refused to give her. Nor would I give her an address. I was in therapy and this is what my therapist suggested.

.   .   .

"YOU HAVE A right to set boundaries," Emily said.

When she said this, I argued with her that it wouldn't work.

"It's impossible," I stated.

"No," she corrected me. "It *feels* impossible."

The feeling was the obstacle. The feeling owned me. She would find me. She would show up. Would I go into the witness protection program?

I WAS COMPELLED to quarantine myself. But I was also compelled to quarantine friends, lovers, acquaintances: the expectation that she would impose and insert herself into my world to get to me made me doubly protective of my life and relationships. She was my problem; it wasn't fair to inflict her on others.

I PROMISED TO call my mother once a week from London, which I did from a pay phone. I called her collect because she insisted this phone call happen.

I was indentured. The money confused me. I accepted help because I needed it. It was a gift, she said. But I knew better. There was no such thing. "I have always been supportive of your dreams and put my money where my mouth is." Reinforcement of the idea that I owed her. And I knew that the expectations would be there no matter what. I was weak.

. . .

I WOULD LEAVE my flat at night in the rain and stand in a red phone booth on a London street corner that smelled of urine.

"I need a phone number for you," she pleaded with me. "I promise I won't use it unless it's an emergency."

I didn't give in. "I don't have a phone."

"How is that possible?"

I made up an excuse.

The excuse was challenged.

The setup: "If you feel in some way I could improve my behavior and be a better mother, please tell me. If you have anything on your mind, don't keep it a secret. I welcome your criticisms, your comments, and your suggestions. You are my child but also my friend and fellow artist. A truthful bond between us means more than anything. I am open to change and it hurts that you don't trust me with your phone number. I know you don't want to hurt me."

I COULDN'T TRUST her with my phone number because I had learned from experience. Phone calls came in the middle of the night. If I didn't want to talk, there had to be an explanation. The explanation wasn't good enough. When caller ID came around, the messages piled up. Messages that went on for ten minutes without her taking a breath.

·   ·   ·

SO I WITHHELD my phone number, but the once-a-week phone calls had to be made. I couldn't take a week off. When I did this anyway, there were repercussions.

"Hello, Ariel," she would say. Flat, cold, battered by my insensitivity. "I waited here for your call last week and arranged my whole evening around it. I waited all night. And the call didn't come. I know that you have no idea what it's like to wait for a call that doesn't come from your child because you don't have a child. But I can tell you that I am fighting despair and sadness that you didn't call me because I am so curious to know what is happening with you. I have you in my mind always because I love you and the very fact that you are you makes me feel good."

Who I am to her is not who I am, and this part of the conversation washes over me.

"Do you think that's a nice way to treat someone? It's very cruel. What happened? Tell me the truth. If you want nothing to do with me and never want to see or speak to me again, tell me."

I couldn't tell her the truth. No one could. Rita's letters are filled with "I couldn't reveal this or she would use it against me." It was mandatory to hold back.

"I was on an assignment," I said. "I was working."

"Well, I'm sure you could have found two minutes to call me and let me know you weren't able to speak."

There was no such thing as two minutes.

"I'm sorry," I said. "It won't happen again."

"You said that the last time. I feel like an idiot. I shouldn't have to beg you to speak to me. It's bad enough that you force me to wait for your call."

Silence.

"Why do you want me to suffer so much?"

I FELT LIKE a bad person. A terrible daughter. And I could not cut off. I wasn't ready. I was afraid of what she would do. The anxiety of not knowing was a threat.

WHEN SOMEONE DOESN'T take no for an answer, you shut the door. But they pound on it. They demand to be let in. The door is shut for a reason. You are bankrupt. You have nothing left to hand over and your pockets are empty. To be on the other side of a door that she couldn't kick in felt unattainable. It was safer to know where she was. Stay one step ahead. She would always be there, kicking and screaming, but it was better this way than to have no idea when she would show up and suddenly, without warning, break the door down.

I LIVED WITH two sets of rules. One for her, one for everyone else. When I was in New York, I couldn't tell her. If she knew I was there, she would insist I spend time with her. I had time for others, why not for her? If I chose not to see her, this led to a maze of conflict that had no exit. It never resulted in "Call me when you feel like it." I walked the streets in Manhattan afraid to run into her. Her claim on me was powerful. I was a master of deception. Did it diminish or exalt me? It didn't matter. I was protecting myself the only way I knew how.

MY INTERIOR CLOCK was set to her mood. When her mood was stable, my life was better. I accommodated that. I believed I owed her. I believed that after everything she'd done for me, everything she'd given me, this entitled her to her due. But there were no limits to her entitlement, and for those in the path of it, there were only two options. Give in or pay a price. I gave in. I wanted a peaceful life and believed this was the only way to get it. These acts of betrayal were self-preservation. Or so I believed.

44

I am sitting alone on the swing outside my office. One of the girls comes over. "What are you doing?" she asks.

"Thinking," I say.

"About what?"

"How to tell a story."

"I love stories," she says. She states that she wants to be a writer like me when she grows up. When the other one sees that her sister has my attention, she comes running across the garden to join us.

"What are you talking about?" she asks.

"We're talking about being a writer."

"Oh, I want to be a writer, too. And a library girl."

"That's a great idea. But it takes a lot of thinking."

"I like thinking!"

"That's good."

The other one adds, "You wanted to be a writer because you love words."

"That's true," I say, taking both of them by the hand. "Let's write some stories."

WE GO INTO my office and I sit at my computer. One of them stands on the left side of my chair, one on the right.

I give them instructions. "Think about what you want to say." They are both silent for a few seconds, and then the one on the left suddenly shouts: "Okay, I'm ready!"

She begins. Once upon a time . . .

As we unfold this tale, she censors herself a few times because she thinks it's not good. I explain she can say whatever comes to her mind. "There is no right or wrong," I tell her. "Your story is beautiful because it comes from you."

I hear myself say this to her. I hear my mother say this to me. She was flawless in those moments. But then she was always using her own poems to illustrate her point. She couldn't help that when she gave, she needed admiration in return.

The other one gets impatient. "My story is ready."

"Okay, you're up," I say. "And then we'll print them out."

As we write these stories, they exude confidence and a belief they have something to say. I don't read them my own poems or share my own stories. I am realizing that I can go with them into their world without needing them to come into mine.

The momentum builds as their stories take shape. There are no limitations. Where will we travel to? What will happen there? There is an exhilaration the three of us share. "Oh, and then . . . and then . . . !" Their excitement is contagious. We take off like a helium balloon headed into the sky.

"Ariel?" One of the girls is poking my arm with her finger. "Can I tell you something?"

Yes, I say, go ahead.

THERE ARE TIMES I will be with the girls and we will be drawing or playing or singing or talking and I am able to rewrite the past. I am seven years old again in the way that it should be. Can I tell you something? Can I ask you something? When they ask me these questions, I respond. They need to be heard.

I will be in the moment but detached from it, too. It is a strange and ethereal feeling. To slaughter the past while replenishing at the same time.

45

I t is time to seek asylum from the barrage of emergencies, the incessant pleas and demands—the quid pro quo bargaining. I am asking for space.

For days, I have spoken about the letter I am about to send my mother but am unable to follow through. "I'm getting there," I've said when Emily asked if I sent it. When Mario asked why I'm waiting. When my father said firmly, "Go for it." I've tried to imagine every conceivable outcome, to map out every way in which she will lash out, envisioning every scenario of how she will respond.

This is the cartography of oppression. To navigate the options, as I have all of my life; to predict the unpredictable. I am good at it. It's a skill I know well. A skill I can rely on to cope with the unknown. But it's a skill that has had side effects, too.

WHAT WILL IT feel like to be free? Will I be free?

February 11, 2014

Dear Mom,

Last week was my 46th birthday. It's taken me all this time to realize my duty now has to be first to myself and my well-being. If you can accept what is good for me, above what you want for yourself, then I believe we can find a way forward.

You say you love me unconditionally. If this is true, you'll let me go. You will understand that I will come back to you in my time, when I'm ready. As you've said, we need different things. You need to see me and speak with me and know where I am; that is not what I want and not what I need.

That is the honesty you ask for. You don't have to tell me how much pain it causes you because I am—and have been for all of my life—informed of your pain and sadness. Your fears and anxieties and insecurities have always been dominant, never been spared. But I am not responsible for your sadness and pain.

THE LETTER GOES on.

It ends with *I hope you don't punish me for my decision, but I can't control how you respond.*

· · ·

THE LETTER HAS been sent. I have blocked all communication from her and from those I suspect will try to reach out to me on her behalf. Whatever stormy response there is, I will not know about it. I will be ignorant of the damage. The suit of emotional armor is on. She can fire but it will not penetrate.

46

For weeks, I noticed a steady decline in his mood. My father was being deflated before my eyes. His heart wasn't pumping properly, and with every passing day, his perspective was changing. Instead of waking up, as he always did, with a cheerful outlook to greet the day, he lay in bed with his thoughts racing, going nowhere, lost in an impenetrable darkness. Anxiety had gripped him. A depression descended. I arrive at his house for breakfast and he looks glum. He talks about not having anything to do, anywhere to go, any friends to visit with.

"I'm frozen," he says, shaking his head.

WE SEE EACH other every day. Our lives are not dissimilar. After breakfast, we separate for a few hours, each of us at our computer in separate rooms, and then we decide where to have lunch. There are four different places we choose from. A local warung that has Padang food is his favorite. Indonesian dishes behind a plate of glass.

We point to what we want and sit down across from each other at a picnic table with locals. He can't twist open the plastic cap on the bottle of water. I watch as he tries, but it won't crack open. "I'm losing my strength," he says softly, shaking his head. His eyes look wearily into mine, and in that moment, my father, the former Marine, is defeated. "No," I say, removing the bottle from his hand, "it's hard to twist it off—even I have trouble."

As the days pass, when I ask "How are you?" he shrugs and forces a smile. "Average." Then, because he doesn't want me to worry, he adds, "I'm okay, I am." But I knew that he wasn't.

His energy was disappearing and he had breathlessness from walking. His pacemaker was overworked. It had to be taken care of. The logistics of this are not simple. His cardiologist in Singapore recommends a cardiac resynchronization therapy device. Every detail of what this means squashes him. Any medical problem requires a trip to another country.

He is frustrated with the failure to regain control. As though he is just now realizing that life ahead of him is maintenance. "I take seven pills a day," he says disapprovingly. "For the rest of my life."

WE SIT TOGETHER in front of his computer and I assist with a transaction online. It requires his password, and when he reveals it to me, I smile. "I use the same word," I say. He becomes emotional and squeezes my shoulder because we're sitting side by side in chairs and can't hug. "We're a team, kiddo," he says. "We're a team."

. . .

SOMETIMES WE'LL BE out to dinner and he is amused to see a group of people sitting together, all of them staring down at their phones, tapping away. We laugh and share disbelief. "It's the end of the world," he says. We will see someone sitting alone laughing out loud, before realizing she is communicating with another human being using the video camera. "Look at that," he says, sighing. It mystifies him, but not really. He reads four different newspapers a day. He is more informed than anyone I know. But his fear and disregard for modern technology has become an attribute that he's attached to himself. He is open-minded about philosophies and ideas, he is a generous and progressive thinker. Deeply analytical. We will have long discussions about a topical event—a trial that is under way or a social injustice—and always during these debates he will say, in a considered and humane way, "Let me be devil's advocate for a second." He sees all sides.

EXCEPT WHEN IT comes to owning a cell phone.

"It's not who I am," he says. I have to accept this. And what this means is that if I want to reach him, I can't. My desire to be in touch with him is trumped by his need to be unreachable. Unwanted communication is an interruption. He is a loner who detoured into a marriage and, when it ended, resumed his resting state of solitude.

. . .

FOR YEARS WE have argued about the cell phone. "You have a daughter," I say. I try to impress upon him that he doesn't have to call me or talk, all he has to do when he is traveling or late for lunch is answer the phone so I know where he's at. My concern is brushed aside.

"If something has happened to me, you'll find out about it eventually. If I'm in the middle of a car accident or having a heart attack, I'm not going to answer the phone anyway."

This "what will be will be" attitude is unalterable. Pushing him gets us nowhere, and he tells me to stop trying to control how he lives and let him be. He senses my frustration and apologizes. "I'm sorry, pal," he says compassionately. "I am who I am."

For a long time I'd believed that his resistance to technology was generational. It is, in part. But the choices he has made from where he lives to how he lives reveal an actuality that defies aging. He is a man who prefers to be cut off.

HE HAS NEVER planned for getting older in a third-world country, even though he has lived in Southeast Asia for over fifty years. Like everyone, he put off what he didn't want to think about. The future. Not being vital. The first time I ever heard my father say "I'm getting old" was in his eighty-sixth year. It was stunning because it was so out of character.

. . .

THERE IS NO infrastructure in Bali that supports Western medical care. He needs medications that are not available in Indonesia, and he will have to go to America. There are details—so many details—to work out. Details that seem insurmountable. Visa agents and paperwork and languages we don't speak. Bali feels like the end of the world.

THE TWO EXTREMES. My mother, who feels entitled to sympathy and has no recognition of being a burden. My father—who doesn't want to impose, doesn't want to encumber me with his problems—has become my biggest worry.

I WALK AROUND his house. It is filled with books. Photographs are in frames. They are either of the two of us, or of him by himself.

A photo in a tent after he climbed Mount Kilimanjaro. He is in his seventies and has a flesh-colored bandage wrapped around his knee. A photo with an orangutan in the jungles of Borneo. He is kneeling down and the orangutan's hand is on my father's upper thigh. A photo of him in a cycling outfit on a mountain bike in Tuscany. And at the top of Gunung Agung, the volcano. There are photos of him trekking in Nepal with a wooden stick, bundled up. It is startling to see my father in winter clothing. I am aware every day of his loss—to have vitality be in the past, knowing it will never be recovered. He is in China. Cambodia. Hanoi. I hold in my hand his medal from the New York City Marathon. His first and only marathon at the age of sixty-four. His name is engraved along with his time: *5.29.37.*

"I'M NOT IN good shape." When he says this, everything stops. There is no wisdom, no time for reflection. There is only a need to fix it and make it better. I feel responsible in a way that I must be. He has no one else.

MY FATHER MAKES lists. It is how he organizes his thoughts. They are written on white notepads and yellow Post-its—hastily jotted down. His handwriting is, like the sound of his voice, characteristic of his stoic manner. He writes trimly and legibly in print that slopes to the right, and the words are recognizable even when he is in a hurry to jettison a thought. The smaller the handwriting, the less integral to his life; but still, it has to be purged. Tiny lettering indicates a reminder of something motivational he knows he should do. Walk!

The lists are all over his desk. Words with question

marks. When something comes up that needs to be tended to, it goes on a list. This is how he talks to himself. He carries a pen and a folded piece of paper in his pocket at all times. Sometimes while we are talking, he will pause to jot down a note. Or he will consult his list to remember something he had to ask me about. It is his way to keep track of the details. He will write down: Batteries for hearing aid. Follow up with Dr. Teo. Follow up about what? The mechanics of his life are a mystery to me. Now the words on the lists are clues to something I must know about.

"IT WAS," HE says, "the hardest decision I ever had to make." He is speaking about why he left New York and moved to Thailand when I was five. It was a painful decision but a decision he does not regret. He could not have survived in New York. He had to be true to himself so that he could be available to me. There are people who cannot withstand conflict and trauma or manage strife. He didn't know what he was getting into. My mother was too powerful. He had to retreat. There was no alternative; he had to disengage. There is no one who identifies with this better than I do. I compensated for the absence of his presence with understanding. He was protecting himself. He had no choice but to leave and I had no choice but to assimilate. I never *felt* abandoned.

·   ·   ·

"I WOULDN'T BE here today and we wouldn't have the relationship we have," he says. He is not a dramatic man. "I would not have survived."

I take his hand and nod. "I know."

"We are a team," he says, with watery eyes. We are a team.

47

The girls have made me Mother's Day cards. One is a colorful drawing of a rainbow with a blue sky and purple stars. The card reads "Happy Mother's Day. I love you Ariel." The other card is in pencil and she has drawn the three of us. The girls have given me these cards without warning. Without fanfare. Mario remarks, "Very colorful," while looking at the card with the rainbow. The other one, whose card is in black and white, appears suddenly in need of approval. In her defense she states, "My hand got tired." That makes me smile.

"I love them both so much," I say, holding the cards in my hands.

WE HAVE A family meeting. It is the night before I leave for New York. I hear a squeak. It might be a rat, but I tell myself it might also be a chirp from a bird. I've learned not to reveal my anxiety in front of them.

Mario explains to them that soon I will be going away for a month. "But you're not going away forever, are you?" one of them asks. No, I say, I am not going away forever.

. . .

EIGHTEEN MONTHS HAVE passed, and I contemplate that
with every ounce of love I give to them, I am rebalanc-
ing the scales. I ask the girls to come into my office so we
can talk. The three of us have special time together. While
Mario is cutting the trees or changing the filter in the fishpond, I tell them how much I love them. I tell them the
cards they made me are my favorite things in the whole
world.

When they are in my office with me we look at the
photos on my desk of when I was their age. They enjoy
this. They remember the stories I've told them. I don't share
the sad stories, only the good ones. One of them points to a
photo of me sleeping while holding my blue rabbit. "That's
Pinky!" she says. Or another one where I am at the table
with my father and Smashy. "That's Smashy!" one of them
says. The other one adds, "You lost him in the taxicab and
your father looked everywhere for him."

"That's right," I say. I feel known.

48

There is a photo of a family. The four of them are in an embrace, the final seconds of a hug, and a moment is captured just before they break apart. It appears the closeness will not be undone. Everyone is smiling in a natural, unguarded way. The handsome father is leaning forward. He laughs, looking down at his two daughters, who are standing in front of him. His eyes appear shut. The woman next to him is leaning back on his shoulder. Her eyes are open slightly and looking straight ahead. Her slender fingers are touching the curve of her neck, as though she has just smoothed away an errant cluster of hair. The two little girls, nearly eight years old, are exactly the same height. Their heads are a few inches below the woman's collarbone. One of the little girls is holding on to her father's forearm, which is wrapped around her torso, and she is hugging it tightly from above and below. Three people are held within the grip of his long arms. Hands, narrow wrists, and fingers in varying sizes are entwined. There is unity.

WHO IS THIS woman in the picture? Was she Photoshopped into it? I look at this image and marvel that it is me. I am here and there, outside and inside. It is incongruous with what I've known. I see stability. I see extradition. I have been repatriated.

I USED TO look at family photos in other people's homes and wonder what it would feel like to be inside of that unity. The vibrations of childhood would disqualify me from that kind of inclusion. I would remain separate.

Because to be separate was to be safe. The destructive beliefs were too entrenched in the landscape of my psyche, rooted in a soil that couldn't be tilled. I believed what was missing would never regrow. Adult life would be recovery from the past. Stasis is all I could have.

"YOU FALL LIKE a sack of potatoes," he says, shaking his head in disbelief and laughing in a caring way. "Why don't you put your arms out to protect yourself?"

Mario is standing on top of a paddleboard. His body is firmly planted like an elegant suntanned statue on the mantel. He holds the paddle in one hand and demonstrates what I should do when I lose my balance. His arm extends in front as he leans forward, mimicking the motion of bracing a fall.

I am several feet away, treading water impatiently. I hold on to the board in front of me with both arms stretched horizontally across it, weary and listless, as though I've been drifting at sea for months. I fumble around for the paddle, which is moving away in the current, and splashing around, I climb back up onto the board.

Later that evening, several hours after the aborted paddleboarding activity, he revisits the fact that I have no reflex to protect myself from a fall.

"I don't understand it," he says. He is trying to figure it out. His voice is soft, but he is stumped. "There was a total lack of response."

MY EQUILIBRIUM IS interior. A refusal to succumb to inherited feelings of helplessness. Equilibrium, for me, was balancing internal conflict. It wasn't possible for my mother to have a feeling and not discharge it immediately. It was up to me to not lose my balance and adjust.

WHEN I LOOK at the photo of the family, I see that I am not condemned. The juggling act in isolation didn't banish me to solitary confinement for life. I am not destroying, in spite of my default to protect myself from harm. The roots of distrust are deep.

But there was a constellation of goodness that provided nurture and built up my resistance. My father. Rita. I can discriminate between what's real and unreal. Satisfaction, which seemed impossibly elusive, is not out of reach.

THE PHOTOGRAPH IS a moment. And I was in it. It wasn't drooping from the weight of the past. Or corroded with anxiety about the future. It wasn't punctured by an urge to sabotage. It is a moment I cherish because it existed. And believing in that moment took a lifetime.

49

I was stamped with disdain for the ordinary. But the ordinary was something I craved. The ordinary is worthwhile, too. Sustaining relationships is ordinary. Not feeling oppressed is ordinary. The odds were flipped. What were the chances I could go against the odds, flatten out a mangled shape, and embrace an ordinary life?

WE WERE SEVEN years old. Christina had come for a play date at 180. It was a bitter cold winter day in New York and we had been playing outside. We took an enormous block of snow, a slab of icy marble, and carried it into the apartment so we could carve it.

"I remember your mother didn't bat an eye," Christina says now. She is seated across the table from me in a noisy restaurant in midtown Manhattan, her fork poised over a plate of mussels. "She was so excited—she said, 'Oh, that's great—put it in the bathtub!' She thought it was the most amazing thing to create something. And I would have *never* been allowed to do that."

I am nodding my head as I listen to her. The permissiveness sounds enchanting.

I can see how my mother's shriek of "Goody!" when she was excited was a welcome alternative to the rules imposed in a functional household. "Going to your house," she adds, "was like going to Disneyland."

Christina talks about how my mother made me take piano lessons. "Your house was always so artsy. Your mom had this kooky sense of humor. I was at a party at your house and had a bug in my glass of water and I said, 'There's a bug in my drink,' and your mother immediately shot back, 'Don't worry, it won't drink much.'"

She laughs at this and mentions she never forgot that line. "I wasn't used to parents talking to children like they were adults. She was sarcastic and I remember thinking, 'She's so cool—she's treating me like an adult.' From the outside, it seemed like she was such a fun, playful parent."

THIS IS THE scene that plays in my head as Christina speaks. A woman has abducted a child. She has hidden the child in the basement. The child is there. A detective comes to the door. He rings the bell, and as this happens, my heartbeat becomes faster, accelerating because I believe the child will be rescued. The circumstances will be revealed and it will all be clear. The child will be released. But when the woman answers the door, she invites the detective inside. The apartment has bookshelves and there are fresh flowers. She charms him. Classical music is playing. She gives him no reason to suspect anything is wrong. She convinces him that she is the victim of a misunderstanding. As this is happening, I want to scream, "No! Don't be fooled! This is not real!" I open my mouth, but nothing comes out. The detective leaves thinking he made a mistake.

I HAVE SEEN my mother crumpled on the floor. She always got up. I have seen her tap-dance with joy. I have seen her tap-dance with sorrow. I've seen her fly a plane, read a poem, captivate a room of people. I've seen her lash out with vituperative fire and unsparing claws. When she felt abandoned. Left out. Not cared for. Living for her was a crisis in progress that had to be shared. An emergency that had to be tended to. A calamity. A threat. A catastrophe. Unaware of the harm she caused to others. She marches on.

THERE WAS NEVER one moment I could point to and say: that's when I knew it wasn't normal. When I was in school or in Thailand, with Rita, my father, or with friends, I knew I felt different than how I felt when I was in my mother's company. Because I wasn't on edge or calculating the best move. But there wasn't a defining incident that marked a clear delineation.

· · ·

THE UNDERSTANDING OF abnormal could only be viewed as an adult, looking back. As a child, there was no barometer for normal other than not feeling under siege.

It could come from being in a plane in the clouds, at the bottom of the ocean, or on an empty road in an unfamiliar neighborhood. These anonymous places where I felt dislocated, off her radar, and undetectable were my sanctuary.

I WAS AT home in this dislocation. Limbo was parole. No verbal or physical attacks. No manipulations. No threats. Removed from the line of fire was as good as it could get. To thrive in those moments was to live in parentheses. Where no one knew where I was. Not even me.

50

It took a long time. Four decades. To learn the damage was not irreparable. To graduate from childhood, where it is no longer an affliction but part of the story, is scaling the wall. Climbing out of the ruins. We tell our stories to be heard. Sometimes those stories free us. Sometimes they free others. When they are not told, they free no one.

THE 79TH STREET crosstown bus is rolling through the park. Central Park West to Fifth Avenue is a stretch of uninterrupted movement I've always enjoyed. The bus doesn't stop to pick anyone up or let anyone off. Even when there is traffic and the bus is at a standstill, this pause is a comfort. Stowed away in a capsule between the East Side and the West Side—between all activity, suspended in timelessness. It has a calming effect. I will get from one side of the city to the other. And in the meantime, there is an acceptable oblivion.

It is the same feeling I have on a flight. Midway over the Atlantic or the Arctic Circle, coasting through darkness. Outside the oval window there is only the abyss. High above earth. I've savored long-haul flights for these interludes. The grinding takeoff, the landing, the stomach-churning turbulence, the crying infant, the hassle, the physical discomfort—all of that fades away during that time when I disappear, surrounded by strangers. Even when I am pinned next to them, I can depart and coast like an astronaut, into another orbit. Weightless.

I DON'T OFTEN take the bus in Manhattan, but the 79th Street crosstown is nostalgia in action. When you grow up in New York City, potent memory is on every street corner, in every neighborhood. I avoid the Upper East Side because of this.

I rode the 79th Street crosstown throughout my childhood, imagining what it would be like when I was older. Passing by the Museum of Natural History, I figured out that in the year 2000, I would be thirty-two years old. That was the same age my mother was when she had me. I don't recall what I was wearing or how I looked or even how old I was when I made this calculation, but the unimaginable prospect of one day being a thirty-two-year-old woman occurred to me on the 79th Street crosstown. One day I would be in charge.

AS I RIDE the bus now, I am between two worlds, two islands. A bifurcated existence.

The juxtaposition is striking. I have removed myself

from everything I knew before. Life has been stripped down to what's essential.

"I CAN'T BELIEVE it," Christina says. I am telling her about my life in Bali over lunch. I tell my friends about it because they are not able to see me in this world. The smells and the sounds of Southeast Asia, the pace and perspective; the life I have with Mario and the girls. The extremity of the change astounds her. She has known me since kindergarten, when I was five.

"When do you go back?" she asks.

"Tomorrow."

She dips a piece of bread into the broth from the mussels. "I knew you wouldn't end up alone."

VICTORY ISN'T THAT I am not alone. It is not letting the aloneness and the aftermath of the past dismantle the present. It is ascending from the depths, not forcing others to join me down there. It is the foreigner in uncharted territory accepting a new and unfamiliar homeland. Can what was learned be undone? Will I permit this internal détente to exist?

Every day is a struggle to fend off estrangement. The unsettled feeling is still there. An ominous sense that I will be disappointed, even though I work to keep it in check. It is an emotional tinnitus muted to a moderate decibel, and sometimes, without warning, it disappears entirely. And in this reprieve there are joyful moments.

Home is not who I was. But the anxiety and detachment is with me no matter where I am. An immutable isolation is the scar tissue. The homelessness is in my bones. In the homelessness, I am at home.

FROM THE BUS, I see people in the city rushing around, buying, consuming. Where are they going? I am sitting near the window and the seat next to me is empty. It is lunchtime on a Tuesday and the bus has a smattering of passengers. It is not crowded. There is the older woman who is smartly dressed with her expensive handbag on her lap. There are nannies and young children. There are students in high school who stare down at their phones.

As the bus comes out of the park and approaches Fifth Avenue, I am still looking out the window when a premonition that I will see my mother seizes me at the exact instant I see her.

MY MOTHER LOOKS disheveled and she is walking slowly. She has a limp. Because of this limp, I feel a surge of sympathy. But she has told me so many times that she is a cripple and can't move, the instinct to feel sorry for her evaporates. She is still moving. The bus stops and I am suddenly struck with panic: What if she gets on? I crouch down in the seat and my adrenaline soars. It is the acute fight-or-flight response—a physiological reaction that grips my nervous system. It tells me I am in harm's way. My heartbeat accelerates. I look for the emergency exit door. It is behind me. Will I be found out? What if she spots me? This response is instinctual. I can relax only once I've located the emergency exit.

I DID NOT hate my mother. I feared her. I feared her destroying my life. I feared her lies would turn others against me. I feared the incessant and unending conflict I would be forced to engage in with someone who couldn't see past her own reality. To put myself first caused her to suffer. I feared the pain I would cause. I feared that pain would metastasize into vengeance. I feared her in the way I did as a child because I was powerless then to protect myself. There are days I am still that child. She frightens me. And her power is undiminished by the passage of time.

SHE IS CROSSING the street and walks on 79th Street between Fifth and Madison. She must have gone for a walk in the park. I watch for a few seconds to make sure it is her. I observe from behind a darkened glass window. I see her, but she doesn't see me.

This is the way it has always been.

51

I'm not changing my story! I'm not!"

I DIDN'T CHANGE my story because my story was real. I knew that at seven years old. My story would not be revised on demand. Even though this demand came from my mother, the person I was biologically encoded to trust. I knew what I knew. In spite of being told my perception was false, or maybe because of it, my experience could not be eroded. The gnarled and deformed words that subverted reality were batted away. This was resilience. A mysterious alchemy of luck, DNA, and outside influence.

THERE ARE STILL days I descend. On these days I am diving alone and no one can reach me. I am out of my depth. I pass twenty meters, pass thirty meters, rapturous with the descent and entering nitrogen narcosis. It's called the Martini effect. But in this instance, the delirium is not a sensation of drunkenness but of nothingness. I descend with abandon, and there is no limit to how far I will go because the ocean I'm in is bottomless.

. . .

MY MOTHER DOESN'T get on the bus. It keeps going and I realize that she is walking slower than the pace at which we are moving. She is looking down at the pavement as she walks. Maybe counting the days until she sees me again. Or fixating on how rotten I am. It could be either. Or both. And what I see is an innocent. She has no idea why I would need to hide from her. She could never hold this in her thoughts. I see her now and there is compassion. What she missed out on and what I missed out on, too. I am grieving for someone who is still alive.

I LOOK AWAY. It is too painful. I am wanting to hug her without wanting her to hug me. She would never let go. Restless, I move seats three times in a matter of seconds. Unconsciously, like a pinball, pinging from one empty seat to the next. The bus stops on Madison Avenue and 79th Street and I jump up out of the seat, forcefully pushing open the exit doors with both arms outstretched as though I am breaking out of the bus, rather than exiting it. I slide past a blockade of strangers and start to run as fast as I can.

I DON'T FEEL my feet on the pavement. I just keep running, tearing away, weaving through cars. I don't stop at the red light. I am compelled to look over my shoulder to see if she is behind me, closing in, but I don't.

My mother could try to chase me, but she won't catch me.

I head downtown on Madison Avenue past the Surrey Hotel, where my father lived; past East 75th Street, where the Hewitt School is still located. I keep moving forward. A long-distance runner through the canyon of childhood. Spurred by endorphins of hope, I outrace the past. Five, ten, twelve blocks pass, and I speed up even though I know I don't have to, enthralled at last by my own motion.

Acknowledgments

THIS BOOK WOULD not exist without the love and support of Rita Waterman.

NO WRITER COULD ask for a more devoted and fierce advocate than David Hirshey. A full-service editor and soul mate in suffering. Thank you for reading every draft, pencil in hand, as though it were the first one. Your friendship, dedication, wicked intelligence, and humor have carried me through. You have stood by my side from the beginning, and I owe you more than a universe of pineapple.

I AM INDEBTED to my very patient agent and friend Rob Weisbach, for his kindness, wisdom, and diplomacy.

MY APPRECIATION AND gratitude extends to Will Blythe. For carving a statue out of the stone and for bringing this book into alignment. Also for judgment I relied on without fail. Thank you for the care and commitment.

THANK YOU AS well to Dani Shapiro, for astute observations and valuable advice at a crucial time.

· *Acknowledgments* ·

.   .   .

I AM DEEPLY appreciative of everyone at HarperCollins. Kate Lyons, for keeping on top of all the essential details and Beth Silfin, for sensitive and undaunted advocacy. And to Sydney Pierce, for being a rock. Special thanks to Michael Morrison and Jonathan Burnham for providing incomparable support in every way throughout the process.

THANKS TO DOUGLAS MACY and MertaSari for the inspirational environment in which to think, swim, and work. And to Emily McGrath, for care and allegiance above and beyond.

THANK YOU TO all my friends for support and encouragement. Laura Belgray, your knowing refrain of "get it done" managed to actually get through.

AND INFINITE GRATITUDE to Mario Bari and the mermaid twins. For providing and steering the ship that helped to heal me.

BOOKS BY ARIEL LEVE

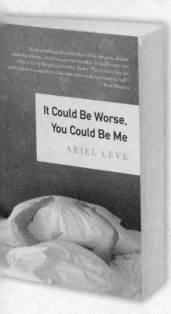

IT COULD BE WORSE, YOU COULD BE ME

Available in Paperback and EBook

"In these bulletins from the front of deepest, darkest curmudgeonliness, Ariel Leve proves herself to be the literary love child of Larry David and Dorothy Parker. This book is like the perfect dinner companion: observant, irreverent and funny as hell."

— Dani Shapiro

"Funny, smart, delightfully cranky"(AJ Jacobs) Ariel Leve's *Sunday Times Magazine* (London) column "Cassandra" moves to book form. *It Could Be Worse, You Could Be Me* offers a humorously bleak perspective on life's potential to turn out badly... and Ariel's innate ability to put the black cloud into the silver lining. This is a book for schadenfreude aficionados; for readers who identify with Cassandra's slogan, "worrying is my yoga"; and for fans of *Difficult People, Girls, 30 Rock*, David Sedaris, Woody Allen, and *New Yorker* cartoons.

1963: THE YEAR OF THE REVOLUTION
How Youth Changed the World with Music, Art, and Fashion

Available in Paperback and EBook

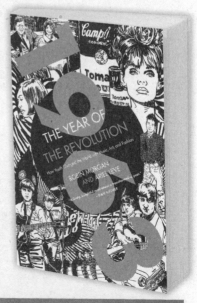

...ively, insightful read about a transformative year."
— Dan Rather

"A vivid and exhilarating guide to the year that ...olutionized pop culture and shook the world, told by the movers and the shakers themselves."

Mick Brown, author of *Tearing Down the Wall of Sound: The Rise and Fall of Phil Spector*

...3: *The Year of the Revolution* records, documentary-...e, the incredible roller-coaster ride of those twelve ...aths, told through the recollections of some of the ...od's most influential figures—from Keith Richards ...Mary Quant, Vidal Sassoon to Graham Nash, Alan ...er to Peter Frampton, Eric Clapton to Gay Talese, ...Stevie Nicks to Norma Kamali, and many more.